LAV

Take Me to Your Government
Four Fables

Count Nef

Drawings by Diana Schuppel

Lytton Publishing Company
Sandpoint, Idaho

ISBN: 9780915728152
Library of Congress Control Number: 2013943171

Take Me to Your Government: Four Fables comprises these
previously published works, revised for this volume:

    Princess Navina Visits Malvolia (1990)
    Princess Navina Visits Mandaat (1994)
    Princess Navina Visits Nueva Malvolia (1999)
    Princess Navina Visits Voluntaria (2002)

Designed by Heather McElwain, Turtle Bay Creative

Many years ago, King Hobart Hollenstein, ruler of the Duchy of Pancratica, sent his heir apparent, the seventeen-year-old Princess Navina, on a world tour to study the governments of other lands. The king believed that the understanding of foreign customs to be gained from such a journey was the best possible preparation for a future monarch. In command of the touring party was the princess's beloved "Uncle Koko," known to the rest of the court as Baron Kolshic, the king's trusted Minister of Cotillion and Foreign Relations. Fortunately for posterity, a record of the journey was kept by Count Nef, a minor member of the entourage. These accounts are excerpted from his personal diary of their travels.

Princess Navina Visits
Malvolia

On the day before we sighted land, our party was seated around the banquette of the *Giovanni* when the baron informed the princess of the next disembarkation on our tour.

"Malvolia?" asked the princess, her brow furrowing. "Why is it called that?"

The baron paused, sighed, then ran his hand through his thinning hair and glanced out at the sparkling sea. "Well," he said slowly, looking back at her, "because it is a land where the monarch wishes his subjects ill. It is apparently his policy to cause harm to his people."

"How horrible!" exclaimed the princess. "But why should I visit such a country?" Then she smiled, "Uncle Koko, do you wish me to learn how to make my dear Pancraticans miserable?"

"Of course not, Navi," he replied, ignoring her playful tone. "We are going to Malvolia so that you may learn what *not* to do as a ruler."

In my opinion, it was a mistake to include Malvolia on our tour. We had learned about its existence from a conversation with a sea captain in Monteriano, and the baron had been intrigued. In a flush of enthusiasm—aided, I fear, by too many glasses of wine shared with that gentleman—he immediately ordered that our party sail thence. I suspect that after a few days he began to alter his opinion about the desirability of visiting so disreputable a land, but he was too proud to admit that his judgment had erred. Of course it was not my place, as the second son of a viscount, to voice my misgivings.

The Malvolian capital of Lamento, its commerce with the outside world being but slight, has no docks or port facilities. We therefore lay at anchor in the harbor for a day, while the baron went ashore to make the necessary arrangements. On the following day, the entire party disembarked for an audience with the magog.

We were apprehensive as we took our places in the long boat. From afar, Lamento looked attractive enough, with quaint, gabled houses nestled at the base of brick-red cliffs rising to an azure sky. But from his visit the day before, the baron had brought back disturbing intelligence of the place. The inhabitants, he had reported, were impoverished to an extreme, and also surly and hostile to visitors. In our anxiety, we found ourselves fingering our scabbards and testing the freedom of our swords as the sailors rowed us across the bay.

At the landing, we saw the truth of the baron's reports, for the site was beset with rag-shrouded beggars, raucously clamoring for alms. As we made our way through the throng, some members of our party gave out small gold pieces, hoping to win the affection of the rabble. Far from appeasing the supplicants, however, these acts of kindness only provoked louder imprecations—some of which reached the ears of the princess herself!

With relief, we gained the security of the carriages and were conveyed thence to the castle—wondering all the while why the magog had permitted a reception so humiliating to the princess, and so discouraging to visitors in general.

The audience with the seventeenth magog of Malvolia took place in the Hall of Mirrors. This vast chamber had no pictures or artwork of any kind. Instead, the walls were covered with many different types of mirrors—long, wide, oval—so that as we walked down the hall to greet the magog, we saw many fragmented images of ourselves moving at cross purposes. It was most disconcerting.

The magog did not lack regal bearing, presenting a well-fed, indeed rotund, figure and wearing a black-and-white–striped zebra cape, and standing tall over his subordinates: It was not until later that we learned this effect was achieved by his underlings standing with their knees always bent.

As the introductions were made, we noted that the baron identified our little duchy as the "Empire of Pancratica." The baron's choice of words puzzled us then, but we were later to see the wisdom of his exaggeration.

After the formalities were completed, the princess began the interview as the baron had instructed.

"Pray tell us, Your Excellency, what kingly principles do you implement in your rule?"

"My dear," replied the magog, pointing his finger at her for emphasis, "in Malvolia we rulers have one principle and one principle only, and that is to make everyone as unhappy as possible."

"I have heard something to that effect," she replied frowning, "but I don't really understand it."

"Sorrow, misfortune, distress," said the magog. "Call it what you will, that is the aim of the magog and of every submagog who serves me. We strive for the greatest misery for the greatest number." He gave a broad smile, obviously unaware how offensive his statement seemed to us.

The princess became agitated. "But why should you adopt such a, such a *frightful* doctri. . . . ?"

The magog held up his hand. "Stop!" he said in a booming voice. "You are guests in our land. You shall not be permitted to abuse our hospitality by questioning our sacred traditions!"

The baron intervened. "We understand, Your Excellency. It is but our purpose to study your institutions, not"—he turned to the princess with a stern glance—"to comment on them." Addressing the magog, he said, "Pray tell us what policies you follow to carry out your goal of making everyone unhappy."

The magog's anger dropped away. His eyes lit up and he rubbed his hands together. "Ah," he said with delight.

"Our policies of the modern era, that is, since my father, the sixteenth magog, differ radically from those of prior generations. The early magogs followed a simple policy. They undertook direct injury of the citizens. Burning was their favorite idea. They would periodically order the soldiers to go out and set fire to crops, barns, and places of habitation.

"These superficial measures did produce some momentary unhappiness, but they had two disadvantages. First, in responding to the adversity thus caused, the character of the citizens was strengthened. They would redouble their efforts and rebuild what had been destroyed. In so doing, they improved their own self-regard and thus laid the basis for their long-run happiness.

"The second disadvantage of the policy of burning was its threat to the dynasty. Because the citizens could see that the magog was directly responsible for the injury, these acts of destruction continually fed the spirit of revolt. Hence, royal burnings could be engaged in but sparingly. Today, of course, we do no burning whatsoever," said the magog proudly.

"How then," asked the baron, "do you make your subjects unhappy—as we have seen they certainly are!"

The magog beamed at this statement, his chest swelling with pride at what he took to be a compliment. "Now we get to the heart of the matter."

He paused for dramatic effect. "Negamos!"

"I beg your pardon?" said the baron.

"Negamos," repeated the magog. "We have adopted the policy of negamos. That is the foundation of misery in Malvolia."

"What, exactly, is a 'negamo'?" asked the baron.

"The name is taken from one of our rivers, Baron. Perhaps I should explain how it came about."

"Please do," said the baron, expressing a curiosity that I doubt he felt.

"It happened in the fall of the twenty-second year of the rule of my father. It was a season of great ferment. My father had carried out some burnings that summer, in fact, quite a bit more than usual. He had destroyed two villages, as well as most of the maize crop. As a result, the citizens were particularly hostile. One afternoon, my father went out in his carriage to survey his holdings in West Nomia. On returning, at the bridge that crosses the Negamo River—actually, the full name is Negamotive—he encountered a band of peasants blocking the way.

"'Give us alms,' they cried. 'We have no food and our houses are burned down.'

"Naturally such words were music to my father's ears, and normally he would have made no move to alleviate the distress he had so carefully cultivated. But the peasants crowded 'round the carriage and began to shake it and beat upon it. My father was reluctant to order his soldiers to disperse the rabble, fearful that an incident of violence might spark a larger rebellion. To ease past this difficult situation, he threw some coins out the window to the throng. The peasants quickly gathered them up, but still they maintained their position blocking the bridge.

"'Why won't you let me pass?' asked my father. 'I have given you the alms you sought.'

"One peasant stepped forward and addressed my father. 'You have assisted us today, but what about next week? Next week you will be fat and warm in your castle and we shall be starving again.' He shook his fist at my father. 'You will forget us.' Thereupon the mob began to rock the carriage from side to side, as if preparing to overturn it! My father shouted, 'No, wait! I shall not forget thee. On my oath as a magog, I pledge that one week hence, I shall return to this very spot. If you are again in want and miserable, I shall again assist you.' Hearing these words, the crowd relented and allowed my father's carriage to escape across the bridge.

"At first, my father had no intention of honoring his promise to return the following week—and, of course, he was in no way bound to do so. In fact, our royal literature specifically counsels against upright behavior. *The Sixth Book of Magogery*, for example, says 'As the alligator sweetly sings, so let the magog's oath be everlasting.'

"But although there was no moral basis to return to the banks of the Negamo, there was a practical one. The kingdom was in a precarious state. Hostile citizens were assaulting his royal officers, even in broad daylight. His spies were bringing in daily reports of conspiracies against the throne. While the state of popular discontent gratified my father's magogic principles, he realized that there were practical limits to idealism. A failure to keep his pledge, he saw, could easily become the spark to ignite a full-scale rebellion.

"On the following Tuesday, therefore, he went back to the Negamo and confronted the crowd—which was much larger than before. 'Are you still miserable and in want?' he asked. At once, members of the crowd began moaning and cursing. 'We have no food,' cried one. 'There is no work in all the land,' shouted another. 'Our clothes are rags,' moaned a third. So again, my father distributed coins, and again promised to return the following Tuesday.

"This continued for many weeks, with my father returning to the Negamo and giving assistance to those who proclaimed their distress. As time passed, the crowd got larger and seemed more and more miserable. The people came in rags and without sandals. Some smeared dirt on their bodies to increase the appearance of suffering.

"Other useful things began to happen. A delegation of farmers came to him to complain about the lack of laborers. Workers, having been given money by my father at the bridge, were not presenting themselves to till the fields and milk the cows. Those that did come were undisciplined and surly, practically daring their employers to discharge them: 'The magog will take care of us,' they jeered at the foremen.

"A delegation of women came from one of the villages to petition about the alms policy. 'Our husbands are becoming shiftless and lazy,' they complained. 'They know they need not work. Now they spend their time with wine and wenches. Their self-respect is dissolving and they grow angry at each other, and at us. And now our sons, seeing no need of mastering a trade, are taking after them.'

"Then my father saw that he had at last achieved what magogs had struggled for generations to accomplish: a durable policy for promoting misery! Even though the revolutionary danger subsided the following spring, he did not cease his policy of returning to the bridge each Tuesday." The magog withdrew an orange handkerchief from his pocket and wiped his brow. "That," he declared, waving the handkerchief with a flourish, "is how the negamo was discovered!"

"I see," said the baron with measured politeness. "Then the negamo is a grant of money, is that so?"

"Not just any grant, my dear Baron," replied the magog. "The negamo is a grant *for being distressed*."

"And do you still go out in your carriage each Tuesday to give out this money?" asked the baron.

The magog laughed. "Goodness no! It would be impossible. We have nearly one million inhabitants in Malvolia, and nearly half receive negamos. No, my father set up a system of booths in the villages where, every Tuesday, all supplicants who deem themselves sufficiently unhappy come to collect their grant. It all works quite smoothly."

At this point, the princess, who had been listening in stony silence to the magog's narration, entered the conversation. She had taken an immediate dislike to the man and had resolved not to flatter him with questions. But now she saw a way to confute him without directly arousing his anger. "But surely," she said, "the people who come for these negamos might actually be quite content. They might simply be pretending to be unhappy in order to collect the money."

The magog was not at all displeased by her question. "Your Princess Navina," he said, winking to the baron, "has the instincts of a true statesman. She knows the tricks that people will play. Yes, my dear," he said, turning back to her, "there was some tendency toward fraud at first. But my father was too clever. He first took jesters with him to the Negamo, to tell jokes and to do tricks, and he watched the reaction of the supplicants. And any who laughed, he sent away without alms. Later, he employed a system of spies and agents to verify that the misfortune of the supplicants was real and not feigned.

"This system of reporting, refined and expanded, is today the cornerstone of the negamo policy. My people do not just play a role of being morose and sullen. They have learned to live it. As a result, even as I peek in windows and spy through hedges to catch people unaware, I can rarely find mirth or enthusiasm in any quarter." The magog beamed proudly, obviously expecting approval.

Our brains were so reeling with the magog's topsy-turvy views that nobody knew quite what to say. Finally, the baron broke the awkward silence. "Your system seems most interesting," he said dryly. "But tell us, how do you finance it? Surely paying all these negamos must cost a great deal of money."

"So far," said the magog, shrugging his shoulders, "the royal mint has been able to keep up. We have just added a ninth stamping machine, which is capable of producing sixty thousand mals an hour. If you have time on your visit here, you really ought to see this machinery."

"Mals?" asked the princess. Her curiosity overcame her resolution to snub the man. "What's a mal?"

"The mal? That's our unit of currency. Page! Show the princess a mal."

The page came forward, bowed to the princess and handed her a coin. It was of dull grey metal and had a skull and crossbones prominently displayed. The princess studied the inscription on the coin. Her brow furrowed. "What is it made of?" she asked.

"Lead," replied the magog, "and 5 percent antimony for hardness."

The princess frowned again. "But it says here, on the coin: 'perfectly pure gold.'"

"So what?"

"Well, I mean, why does it say it's gold if it's lead?"

The magog shrugged. "I suppose that it's just traditional. The earlier mals, before the days of my father, were made of gold and we have kept that inscription. Surely it doesn't matter. Money is just a medium of exchange. It's just superstition that money ought to be gold or silver or something valuable like that."

The princess said nothing, but it was clear that she was not satisfied.

"And besides," continued the magog, "we couldn't possibly make our mals out of gold. There wouldn't even begin to be enough. You see, we have to constantly increase our production of mals. It's the only way to keep up with the great inflation we have here."

"Inflation?" said the baron.

"Yes indeed, my dear Baron. Since the days of my father, the price of everything has risen enormously. No one seems to understand why. A loaf of bread, for example, used to cost two mals. Now it's over two hundred. This inflation makes it necessary to increase the negamo time and again, or it would cease to serve its purpose. Over the past 55 years, the negamo has been raised from 13 mals to 1,200—actually it is 1,225 this week. Obviously, to cover this increase, we must increase our production of mals. Of course," the magog added as an afterthought, "we do get some income from the prosperity fines, but that's hardly significant."

"Did you say 'prosperity fines?'" asked the baron.

"We call them prosperity fines, Baron, but I prefer to think of them as dreaming fines," replied the magog. "You cannot measure their contribution to unhappiness in terms of the mals taken from the populace."

"I'm afraid I don't understand," said the baron. "I haven't heard of a prosperity fine before."

"My goodness, your system of political economy must indeed be backward if you have not heard of a prosperity fine," said the magog. "For us, the idea originated with the third magog. In many ways, the discovery of this policy took the same path as the discovery of the negamo. It was a temporary expedient to combat rebellion, which was later retained for its long-term advantages." The magog interrupted himself to snap his finger at a page. "The sillonte!" he hissed at a page boy.

The page rushed to the side of the hall and, assisted by another, brought a golden throne-like chair for the magog to sit upon. The magog had obviously grown tired of standing on his feet. Just as obviously, he had no concern for the discomfort of his guests who were forced to remain standing.

"Ah, that's better," said the magog, relaxing back into the sillonte and stretching out his legs. "As I was saying, the prosperity fine began as a strategy by the third magog to divert hostility from the dynasty. He went out and told angry workers and peasants that the real reason they lacked food was not due to the royal burnings. Instead—he told them—it was the wealthy who were responsible for their poverty. 'Their barns are bulging with corn,' he declaimed, 'and they burn wheat in their ottavars to spite the misery of the people. Is this just?' Of course the crowd thought not, and the magog made a pledge to them: 'Upon each of the rich shall I levy a fine, each fine in due proportion to the income of each. And the funds thus raised I shall distribute unto you.'

"It was another rare instance in the history of Malvolia when a magog actually kept his promise. The magog confiscated the property of the wealthy in proportion to their income, and distributed some of the proceeds to the people. When the rebellion passed, he stopped the distribution, but he retained the system of proportional fines for its beneficial effect in vexing the wealthy.

"Later, in the fifteenth century, the great social philosopher, Nauseo the Elder, discovered more profound benefits of the prosperity fine. He pointed out that it discourages production, innovation, and saving. You see, with the fine, people are progressively penalized for making more income. That is, they are penalized for whatever creative work they do: raising corn, making watches, building dontiefs. So the country gets less work, less production.

"But"—the magog was perspiring with the enthusiasm of his narration—"that isn't all. Nauseo pointed out that there was a hidden depressing effect of the prosperity fine, an effect on dreams and aspirations. You see, for everyone who actually succeeds in any risky, difficult venture, there are thousands who are only dreaming about such conquests. They are kept going by the slim hope that they, too, might make their dream come true. There are farmers hoping to develop a supermaize; inventors pursuing the possibility of a flying machine; writers scribbling away in their garrets, aspiring to write the great Malvolian novel. Their dreams and hopes give them a sense of purpose.

"The prosperity fine undermines these dreams. It makes it impossible to dream of future wealth. The individual knows that even if he succeeds, and his project becomes highly profitable, the government will rob him of the fruits of his labors. As a result, creative and energetic people in Malvolia are particularly frustrated and morose. Really," the magog shifted his gaze to the baron, "if you don't have a prosperity fine in your Empire of Pancratica, you surely should get one!"

The magog again blotted his forehead with his orange hand-kerchief. He assumed his listeners were dumbfounded with admiration. "The manner in which we collect the prosperity fine," he continued, "adds a further nuance of frustration. We require that each person calculate his own fine, which might not be too difficult, except for one thing." He paused, his eyes brimming with sneaky delight. "The rules and regulations for computing the fines are immensely complex and illogical! This means that everyone has

Malvolian Dontief

to work long and hard to try to figure out his fine, always haunted by the fear of doing it incorrectly and going to jail.

"So you see," he said, sweeping his arm in another of his grand gestures, "we have at last contrived the perfect administration of unhappiness here in Malvolia. Our less energetic citizens are maintained in idleness and despair through the system of negamos. And they blame their misery not on the dynasty, but on the more productive citizens who, in turn, are harassed and frustrated by our prosperity fine. Discontent prevails at all levels, and yet our dynasty remains unchallenged."

"Are there no revolutionaries in Malvolia?" asked the baron.

"Not to any significant degree," replied the magog with a deprecating wave of his hand. "Of course, there are always a few hotheaded lads, but they have no following among the people."

The princess could contain herself no longer. Under her breath, she made a sound.

"What was that, my dear?" asked the magog. He had failed to detect her growing hostility.

"Shocking!" exclaimed the princess in a louder voice. The baron gave her a warning glance, but she was too upset to heed him. "What you are doing to your people is simply shocking!" She stamped her foot.

The magog's eyes bulged as he grasped the meaning of her words. "In Malvolia, it is a capital offense to contradict our philosophy." He waved to the soldiers standing along the wall. "Guards! Arrest Princess Navina!"

The baron quickly stepped toward the magog. "Stay a moment," he said, holding up his hand. "Your Excellency would be most illadvised to take action such as this. Such a deed could easily end in war with our empire."

"War?" said the magog, glowering back at the baron. "What care I about war? All that would do is make my people more miserable. I would welcome a war with your Empire of Pancratica."

"But," said the baron, "surely you must realize that this war, if it should come about, would produce the destruction of your dynasty. When the empire I represent defeats you, we would certainly replace you with rulers who had the welfare of the Malvolian people at heart."

"Ah," said the magog, lowering his voice and frowning. "That would indeed be distressing." He paused. "But how would your empire fight such a war in any case? Your brigantine in the harbor, I am told, is unarmed."

The magog was correct on that point. The Duchy of Pancratica, being landlocked, has no navy at all. The vessel in which we sailed had been hired from a merchant firm in Genoa. The baron was indeed in a close pass. But he was equal to the challenge.

"Your Excellency, we are but the advance messenger of the Pancreatic armada. In three days, they will overtake us and then you will see the Bay of Lamento white with sails of our warships!"

The vividness of the baron's image caused the magog to hesitate. Pressing his advantage, the baron made a proposal. "But let us not talk of war, Your Excellency. We have come to study your institutions. Surely you have more points to explain?"

"Yes indeed!" The magog's anger fell away. "I particularly wanted the princess to learn about how we promote social conflict. I was going to explain the subject tomorrow."

"There. You see?" said the baron. "I am sure the princess is most eager to learn about such things—and she could hardly do so if she were, er, confined. Why don't we, therefore, postpone this other matter until the armada arrives, and continue with the visit as planned?"

The magog pondered the baron's words, and then nodded his head in agreement. "Very well," he replied. "But I must warn the princess not to repeat her outburst. Here in Malvolia you can criticize our policies, but not our assumptions."

The princess nodded stiffly, forcing a smile. On this uncertain note, the audience with the magog was concluded.

As we walked back to the main gate of the castle, the princess whispered to the baron, "I hate that man! Mean to everybody—and mean to us, not even giving us chairs to sit on. And he has such *dreadful* taste. Imagine, an orange handkerchief! Uncle Koko, let us go to the ship and sail at once."

"No, my dear," cautioned the baron in a hushed voice. "We are being watched. If we make any attempt to flee, the magog will know that my story of the armada is a bluff, and we shall all be arrested at once. No, we must continue with the visit quite naturally and wait for an opportune moment to slip away."

The princess bit her lip.

The Misery of "M"

The lodgings that the magog had arranged for us at the Olde Ache Royal Hostel were not entirely to our liking. The rooms were bare, damp, and musty smelling, and the tiny windows refused to open. Particularly irritating were the water faucets. When opened, no water came out. Naturally, after trying them, one left them open. Later, when one had forgotten, the water suddenly surged out with enormous force, splashing across the room and drenching whoever approached to close the faucet. When turned on a few moments later, water would again refuse to flow.

In the room reserved for the princess, she found an enormous bed covered with a down mattress fully five feet thick. When she first pressed her hand on it, she exclaimed with delight at its softness, praising it over the sturdy bunks of the ship. She was to regret her words, however. When she tried to sleep on it, she sank so deeply down that the mattress engulfed her and made her perspire. Furthermore, her arms and legs were pinned in the deep cleft of the mattress, so she could not stir or turn in any direction. Many times during the night, she struggled out of the bed to pace the floor, only to be driven back to her feather prison by the sound of mice scurrying across the floor.

After passing such a night in this abominable hostel, the princess was understandably not in the best of humor when we returned to the castle the next day.

The magog again received us in the Hall of Mirrors, seated comfortably on his gilded sillonte. He turned to address the princess.

"And how did you pass the night, my dear?" he asked with a wide grin. He seemed to have forgotten his anger of the day before.

The princess, showing her good breeding, only said, "Very well, thank you."

The magog seemed disappointed. "Really? Are you sure there wasn't some discomfort?"

"Well, if you really want to know," said the princess hotly, "I spent the most disagreeable night of my life in that horrid bed!"

"Just as I expected," said the magog, slapping his thigh with delight.

"You mean you knew I would be uncomfortable?"

"But of course!"

"Why did you permit such a thing, then?"

"My dear, this is Malvolia. It is my duty to make everyone, even visitors, unhappy."

The princess stamped her foot. "Well, why didn't you just . . . just burn the hostel down if you wanted to make me unhappy?"

The magog was undisturbed by her petulant tone. "Ah, my dear, a fire would have been so old-fashioned, and also counter-productive. Suppose that you had escaped with your life. Then you would have had a delightful tale of adventure to recount to your children and grandchildren, making them, and you, happy in the telling of it. But what tale is there to tell about passing an uncomfortable night in a bed too soft?"

"But suppose I died in the fire?" asked the princess.

"Then you would be dead, not unhappy. Dead people are not unhappy. For this reason, in Malvolia, we avoid killing any-body, except, perhaps, visitors who contradict our philosophies"— he looked pointedly at the baron—"without armadas to back them up."

The baron stepped forward. "Be that as it may," he said, and quickly changed the subject. "We understand you wished to explain your policy of social conflict today. We are most anxious to learn of your treatment of this problem."

"Yes, indeed," replied the magog, apparently forgetting his threat. It seemed that whenever he turned to discussing policy, the magog became a changed man, fully engrossed in the delights of administrative theory.

"Our policy began with the fourteenth magog. He had learned from travelers about the problems with minorities that existed in the Austral-Hungovian Empire." He turned to the baron. "You have heard of that kingdom?"

"It is a small realm lying to the southwest of our empire," said the baron, always careful to sustain the image of Pancratica's greatness.

"The fourteenth magog learned that minorities—Saxons, Jukes, and such—were a great source of misery in that kingdom, always squabbling with each other and resenting each other, and naturally he wondered if it wouldn't be possible to bring this problem to Malvolia."

"Naturally," echoed the princess, but the magog missed her sarcasm.

"Unfortunately, Malvolia does not have any natural social divisions. Everyone here speaks the same language and shares the same culture and religion. Therefore, in order to create social conflict, the magog saw he would need to create an artificial minority.

"He began with the ems, that is, everyone whose last name begins with the letter M. All such people were made the object of special oppressive legislation. They were not permitted to attend the university; they could not ride in the public dontiefs; they were forbidden to take part in the professional dugeball contests; and they had to pay a special yearly fine of, if I recall rightly, 12 mals.

"Of course, the ems were injured by these measures, and to this degree one could say the policy succeeded. But, as often happened with ancient magogian policies, there were unintended side effects that counteracted the original intent.

"First, in order to overcome the disadvantage laid upon them, the ems became particularly industrious. They worked longer hours in the shops and fields, and trained their children to be frugal and hardworking. Thus, they developed healthy attitudes that laid the foundation for their future success.

"Second, many non-ems began to sympathize with the ems. Some non-ems went out of their way to employ ems, others helped to found and sustain the Em University, and many took up a campaign against the dynasty to repeal the laws against ems. In this way, sentiments of brotherhood and cooperation began to develop.

"Matters continued in this unsatisfactory state until my father, the sixteenth magog, took up the issue. He had discovered, with his negamo, the great principal of social decay, that misery is fostered by a regularized system of granting unmerited benefits. He applied this insight to the minority issue, and realized that he needed to reverse the existing policy. He abolished all oppressive legislation and replaced it with positive measures designed to confer an advantage on ems. He instituted a fine of 70 mals against anyone who failed to give employment to an em. He reserved 200 places at the University of Malvolia for em students. And he began a special, extra negamo, called the "negamem," of six mals, given only to ems.

"As a result, the ems now look to the dynasty, instead of their own efforts, for their social improvement, and expend their energies, constantly agitating for an increase in the negamem."

"But surely," asked the baron, "the ems are aware of their special treatment, are they not? They must see through this effort to subvert them."

"Yes and no, Baron. They are aware of the special legislation, but they view it as a just corrective for their special circumstances." He adopted a didactic tone. "One must never underestimate a group's capacity to believe that it suffers a special disadvantage requiring governmental redress."

The cynicism of the magog's declaration rendered us speechless, but, as usual, he failed to detect our uneasiness. "This is not to say we have rested on our laurels creating social conflict," he rushed on. "Some years ago, the ens began agitating to be included under em legislation, arguing that they resembled ems and faced similar problems. So we extended the policy to them. Next January, we will extend the policy to ohs and pees. It is our long-run objective to turn all our citizens into governmentally supported minorities, with each resenting the subsidy given to the others!"

He turned to the baron. "If you stay in Malvolia long enough, Baron," he said with a wink, "we shall get around to you with the letter K."

The baron smiled at the jest, but he caught the barb that lay behind it. "Most interesting indeed, Your Excellency." He made a show of consulting his gold pocket watch. "My goodness," he exclaimed, "I'm afraid it's time to conclude our audience. The princess is much fatigued and . . ."

The magog appeared to accept the point. "But you will return tomorrow to see our mint?" he asked.

"Oh, yes, indeed," replied the baron. "We wouldn't want to miss seeing your new stamping machine."

A Malvolian Revolutionary

Thus we took our leave of the magog once again. The royal party repaired to the hostel to review a situation that was growing more desperate by the minute. There was no Pancreatic armada, of course, and the magog was becoming ever more skeptical of the baron's bluff. It seemed only a matter of time before we were all arrested and perhaps even executed by the villain who ruled this forsaken land.

Shortly after sunset, our fortunes took a turn for the better. There entered the hostel a youth, a handsome young man with long, wavy golden hair and proud bearing, dressed in workman's garb that was obviously new, with unnecessary new patches sewn over the knees of the overalls. He asked to see the princess. He had, he said, a message concerning her safety that he would deliver only to her. His request was unusual, but so were our circumstances. After some hesitation, the baron sent for the princess and she came down the stairs to the main hall where our party had gathered.

He introduced himself to her, bowing slightly. "My name is Lare Bil, Your Highness. I am a junior tutor at the university and have donned these rustic garments as a disguise. I come to warn you that you are in the greatest danger. The magog intends to arrest you and your entire company this very night!"

"Oh dear," said the princess. "What shall we do?"

Before the youth could speak, the baron interposed. "How do you know this, and why have you taken the trouble to warn us?"

"I am the leader of the Committee for Deconstructing Malvolian Dysfunctions," he replied. "We are enemies of the magog and are sworn to overthrow him. We learned of his intentions against you from one of our spies in the magog's castle.

"You must flee to your ship at once," he continued. "The magog has posted guards in front of the hostel, but you may escape through the coal cellar. I can lead you through the back alleys so that you may reach your ship before he learns of your escape. But you must hurry!"

There seemed to be no alternative but to trust him. Orders were given to prepare for our departure from the hostel. While the trunks were being packed, the princess engaged the young man in conversation.

"It is very good of you, and brave of you, to help us in this way," she told him. "You seek to overthrow the magog, do you?"

"Yes, Your Highness. We shall not rest until the dynasty is destroyed."

"I do admire you for it," she replied. "No undertaking could be more noble than to put an end to that horrid man's rule! Tell me, Lare, what policies do you intend to follow after you have overthrown the magog?"

His face lit up with enthusiasm. "We have discussed this question night after night at our meetings at the university. Our first and most important measure, when we come to power, will be to *increase the negamo!*" He thumped his fist on the table. "As it is today, the people of Malvolia are practically *starving* on the negamo of 1,225. Why, with inflation being what it is, 1,225 mals is barely enough to keep body and soul together."

"Bravo, young man!" This comment came from Count Zinn, a minor member of our traveling party. The count breaks out in rather strange enthusiasms that we have, for the most part, learned to humor.

"Yes, indeed!" continued Count Zinn. "If you give the people of Malvolia enough money, they will be happy, and this will defeat the evil purposes of the Magog!" He slapped his thigh in excitement. I looked at the baron and rolled my eyes.

"I see," said the princess to Lare, ignoring the count's interjection. "But tell me, how do you intend to pay the cost of this increased negamo?"

"We have thought of that, too," he replied. "We shall enact a tax on the wealthy, a tax that increases in proportion to each person's income."

She frowned. "But doesn't the magog already tax the wealthy?"

"Oh no, no, no. Not at all! He has a system of *fines*. We are talking about a *tax*."

"What's the difference?" asked the princess.

"Well, it's . . . it's obvious. A fine . . . I mean . . . a fine is *unfair*. A tax is *fair*."

I could see from the expression on the princess's face that she was far from convinced, but she did not want to discourage the

young man. "Well," she said, "I do agree that something needs to be done about that man's evil policies."

At that moment, the conversation had to be interrupted by our departure. Lare led the princess and the rest of our company to the basement and out through the coal cellar. Wriggling out the narrow chute begrimed our clothes with carbon, but this was a small price to pay for our safety. Ever so quietly, walking carefully on our toes, we followed our guide through a series of twisting alleys and paths. Soon we reached the beach where the long boat, unguarded, was lying drawn up on the sand.

Before she climbed aboard, the princess turned to Lare. "May God go with you," she said, looking into his eyes. Then she stood on her tiptoes and surprised the lad with a quick kiss on the cheek.

As soon as we reached the brigantine, the anchor cables were cut and we glided out of the harbor to the open sea. The princess remained standing by the taffrail, waving, until all sight of land was gone.

Before retiring, we all toasted our deliverance from the accursed land of Malvolia with a double measure of carbingac.

The next morning, the baron and I were taking the sea air at the windward rail when the princess came on deck and joined us. She stood quietly for some time looking at the sea, watching the seagulls dodge and dart over the heaving swell.

"Uncle Koko," she said suddenly. "What's the difference between a fine and a tax?"

"Well, er, I suppose one could say that a fine is unfair while a tax is fair."

"Yes, that's what Lare said," replied the princess. "But why?"

The baron thought for a moment. "It's a question of motive, really. A fine is a type of punishment. The ruler who wishes to harm his subjects, like the magog of Malvolia, uses fines. The ruler who seeks to improve his kingdom uses taxes. For example, your father collects a ten dina tax from all who enter the royal capital city of Plotz. He collects this money not as a punishment—for he loves his subjects—but in order to maintain the royal stables. It's all a question of intentions."

"Hmm," said the princess slowly, her eyes gazing on the sea.

We stood in silence for a time, watching the gulls skim the waves. Then the princess addressed me. "Count, how can I send a letter to Lare?"

"Do you know his address, Princess?" I replied.

"Yes, he gave it to me last night, and I have put it on this letter here." She showed us a letter already sealed and addressed. "I have written him to encourage his efforts, and to urge him to study the background of Malvolia's policies, so that he understands their real nature.

"What I fear," she continued, "is that this letter won't be delivered. In that horrible Malvolia, they will reason that since a letter might give the recipient pleasure, it must be denied him."

"A very good point, Princess," I said as I pondered the problem a moment. In a flash, I saw the solution. "May I have the envelope, please?"

She handed it over and, laying it upon the binnacle, I wrote an additional message upon it in a clear, bold hand:

Warning! Contains tragic news.
Do not open if discouraged or depressed.

When the princess saw it, she astonished me with a hug, and said—these were her exact words—"Count Nef, you are a prodigy!"

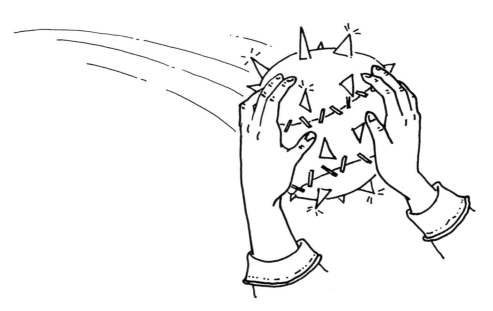

Malvolian Dugeball

Princess Navina Visits
Mandaat

"I'm afraid I have very little additional information about the place." The baron was addressing us as we sat after dinner around the supper table of the *Giovanni* on the eve of our arrival in Mandaat.

He spread a rumpled parchment letter out on the table before him. "All my correspondent says," he continued, putting his finger under a line of text in the document, "is that in Mandaat, 'legislation is the leading industry, and, as a result, they have a plentitude of laws.' He cautions us that, before we undertake any action, we should question the natives about its permissibility." The baron raised his head and looked pointedly at the princess.

She accepted the justice of his implied rebuke. She was quite aware that it had been her bold outspokenness that had placed us in such a dangerous situation in Malvolia. "I'll try to be more careful, Uncle Koko," she said. "But sometimes I just can't keep what's inside me, well, inside."

The baron smiled indulgently, for he recognized the princess's independent spirit, and the group returned to enjoying the after-dinner carbingac and cheese. I was not easy, however, and suspected that we had not seen the last of complications from the princess's unguarded expressions. Having been raised from an early age by tutors and governesses who feared to contradict her, she was used to frankly voicing her opinions.

We had no difficulty berthing our brigantine in the harbor of Mussen, the capital of Mandaat. The city lies at the edge of a gradually rising plain; in the very great distance in the sparkling clear air, we could see the snowcapped peaks of the cordillera.

We made our way down the gangplank onto the cobblestone quay and were surprised to find no one about: no welcoming party, not even passersby whom we could question. The streets were entirely deserted. After pondering this puzzling situation, the baron decided that we should walk to the governmental palace, an imposing edifice standing less than two furlongs up the main avenue from the harbor.

No sooner had we begun our stroll than we heard the shrill hooting of a horn, which sounded not unlike the calling of a crow. Following the sound to its source, we saw a short man dressed in a black uniform scurrying down a side street to meet us, blowing his raucous horn all the while. Our first thought was that this official was delegated to welcome us to the country. This was a misjudgment.

"Your mandates please," he said in an abrupt tone. He was breathing heavily from his dash to intercept us.

"I beg your pardon," said the baron.

"Mandates! Show your mandates! What are you waiting for? I am a very busy person!"

"I'm afraid we don't understand," said the baron. "We are voyagers who just . . ."

"Not again!" said the official, casting his eyes skyward in a gesture of great exasperation. "I spend half my time explaining these regulations to new entrants. It really would be simpler," he continued, looking out at the sea, "if we just prohibited travelers altogether." He turned back to the baron. "To use the streets anywhere in Mandaat, you must have a mandate. That's all."

"And what, pray, is a mandate?" asked the baron.

"It's a document, a license, which gives you permission to use the streets. It says where you are going *from*, and where you are going *to*, and *when* you are making the trip. No one can be on the streets without one. So get back there." The official poked his club at us in a threatening manner, so that we were forced to retreat back onto the quay.

"But why do you have this law?" asked the princess.

The official regarded her with scorn and impatience.

"Even a fool can see the necessity for it. Why, if you didn't regulate the streets, people would go where they wanted when they wanted, and they would bump into each other and hurt each other. The result would be complete chaos. Mandates keep people from using the same part of the street at the same time."

"But couldn't people avoid hitting each other when they walked on the streets?" persisted the princess. She asked the question politely, but the official grew even more impatient.

"It's obvious you know nothing about human nature, missy! You have no idea how stupid and selfish human beings can be when left free to act on their own." He looked back at the baron. "Anyway, I cannot waste time discussing it. Wait here until you get your mandates." With that, he turned on his heel and strode away.

Our astonishment at this bizarre custom of Mandaat gave way to a sense of frustration, for we were trapped by a logical impossibility: Lacking mandates we could not go anywhere to find out how to get mandates!

Several hours passed as we waited impatiently on the quay. Finally, we spotted a party of officials leaving the governmental palace and making their way down the long avenue toward us. This proved to be the welcoming party we had expected.

The leader was a tall, elderly gentleman of distinguished bearing who introduced himself as Dr. Amos Doasdo. He greeted the princess and the baron. "I am so sorry that you had to wait," he said, making a pained grimace. "We had the greatest difficulty getting our mandates today; otherwise we would have been here in plenty of time to meet you."

"But why do you have these things, these 'mandates,' if they are so inconvenient?" asked the princess.

Dr. Doasdo looked at her with alarm. "Oh, you couldn't do without mandates. What's a little inconvenience now and then for a system that prevents chaos? Mandates are the price we pay for civilization."

"But . . ." The princess interrupted what she was going to say, having caught a warning look from the baron. Perhaps, I thought, she had learned some self-discipline from that scrape in Malvolia after all!

Dr. Doasdo had brought mandates for everyone in our party to enable us to proceed to the governmental palace. The mandate is a triangular placard that dangles from a chain hung around the neck. It is deliberately large so that its presence, or absence, can be detected at a great distance by the commissioners, the officials who enforce the mandate laws. As we began to walk, we found these devices banged against our knees in a most irritating fashion.

Lodgings had been arranged for us in the Grand Governmental Supreme Palace, as it was called, so that we would have no need of mandates to pass from our sleeping quarters to the offices of government. After a period of rest and unpacking, it was time for the first inspection on our tour, a visit to the legislative body, the Salon die Reglement. Dr. Doasdo had felt that it was most important for us to stop here first. "Here is the heart, and soul, and brain of the country," he said, as he ushered us through the massive door of the visitors' gallery. "This is what makes society function."

We took our seats on the plush red velvet chairs and inspected the strikingly opulent fixtures and furnishings of the gigantic chamber. The entire north wall was a mural, intricately crafted, depicting a burly soldier lifting a rather plump, and somewhat muddy, maiden from a ditch. The caption below read "Authority Exalts Compassion." The ornaments, statuary, paintings, and gold leaf bespoke fabulous sums spent on decorations.

Our expressions of astonishment at the display of grandeur were cut short by a monitor who came down the aisle and insisted upon our silence.

We turned to listen to what the orators were saying. The words were incomprehensible.

"Yv xzfgrlfh rm zhhfnrmt blfi mvrtsyli'h rmgvmgrlm gl wl szin," said one.

"Bvh, yvxzfhv gsv yvorvu rm srh vero rmgvmgrlmh droo qfh-grub gsv fhv lu ulixv ztzrmhg srn," said another.

"What language are they speaking?" the baron asked the doctor.

"That is Liberta."

"Do they understand it?"

"Of course not. Liberta is a long-dead language, used by the ancient tribes of this land. To honor our ancestors, we have passed a law forcing people to speak this language on certain formal occasions like meetings of the Salon die Reglement."

"But then, how do legislators communicate with each other?" asked the baron.

"Well, here, actually, they don't," replied the doctor. "You see, what is said in the Salon is mainly for display. The real work of the body takes place in the committees. That is where the reglamentarians discuss the laws that are voted on."

The doctor then pointed to a tall stack of paper standing on a sturdy metal platform. "See, that is the bill they are voting on today. It is the Trifle Regulation Act, number 10,663. We try to have at least three or four of these every year."

"Isn't that a scale it is standing upon?" I asked.

"Why, yes, it is, Count," replied the doctor. "How clever of you to notice! Yes, we weigh all our legislation here. That is how we evaluate our progress. Last year the Salon approved 29.3 tons of laws, nearly a ton more than last year. That is how reglamentarians appeal to the public, saying how many pounds of laws they proposed, and how many pounds of their proposed laws were approved by the Salon. If the voters think their contributions have been weighty enough, they reelect them."

"Are these gentlemen able to read the laws they are approving?" asked the princess. "Why, that pile alone must be four feet high."

"Of course not," replied the doctor. "No human being could read so much."

"But shouldn't they understand the laws they are approving?"

"My dear, that would never do. If they waited until they knew what they were voting on, they would never get anything done."

At that moment, the monitor returned and scolded us for talking. The doctor decided it would be best to exit and continue the conversation in the hall.

Once the gallery door had closed behind us, the princess spoke. "But surely it's silly for people to pass laws they don't know anything about. When I become queen of Pancratica, I'm going to read all the laws I approve."

The doctor seemed offended by her remark, but he maintained a civil, if stern, tone in replying. "You fail to understand, Miss, the real purpose of legislation."

"Isn't it to make things better?" asked the princess.

"Ha!" he said with a smile breaking on his face. "That is precisely where your thinking goes astray. The passage of laws has almost nothing to do with making things better. The real purpose of legislation is . . ." he paused for emphasis, "reassurance." The doctor had regained his genial tone as he moved onto what was for him obviously familiar ground.

"You see, human beings are a naturally frightened species, afraid of things outside their understanding and control. They need to believe in some power capable of knowing about and commanding these worrisome objects. In some societies, they have what are called 'witch doctors,' who wave colored flags at the sun. Here in Mandaat, our reglamentarians perform this function. They reassure the populace that they are in control of strange and menacing phenomena. The key to this role is being energetic, busy. After all, what would people think of a witch doctor who waved a flag at the sun only once a year? So you see, that is why the passage of a large volume of laws is so important, and why the reglamentarians don't need to understand their content."

There was an awkward silence after this statement by Doctor Doasdo. Because he had spoken with such authority, no one cared to question him further. The doctor's official post, as he had explained to us during our introductions that morning, was that of Justificator. It was his duty to explain to visitors and critics, concerning every aspect of the regime of Mandaat, that whatever is, is right.

Being lunchtime, we were conducted along the corridors of the Supreme Palace to one of the many dining rooms located in the building. This room was decorated in the same lavish style as all other parts of the palace, with intricate plaster moldings and highly polished inlaid wood flooring. Apparently, whoever suffered in Mandaat, it was not officials of the regime.

When we were seated, the waiters brought our plates containing a meat prepared according to a style they called a la Chateau D'if, and a puree of potatoes. After all the plates had been laid before us and no one had begun to eat, the princess took up her fork, assuming that it was her role to commence.

The doctor gently rested his hand on her elbow. "I'm afraid we must wait, Princess." The princess put down her fork, blushing in embarrassment.

Several minutes passed. Finally, the princess asked, "What are we waiting for?"

"For the meat and potatoes to be inspected," replied the doctor. "It is one of our laws that no one may eat meat or potatoes in any restaurant unless it is approved by a government inspector after it has been served."

The doctor turned to the rest of the party. "You may, however, eat bread and drink water. These do not need inspection." He dropped his voice, looked cautiously to one side, and added, "Yet."

He took up a roll and beckoned us to do likewise. "Feel free," he said. "Feel free." We noticed then that the people sitting at the tables around us were eating only bread and drinking only water, while their plates of meat and potatoes were untouched.

"What is the point of this inspection law?" asked the princess.

"Why, of course, it's to keep the restaurant from serving tainted or poisonous food," replied the doctor.

"But why don't you just inspect the restaurant generally? Why must you inspect every single plate when it's served? Can't you depend on the cooks and waiters not to serve food if it is obviously bad?"

"Oh, dear no. You have no idea how stupid and selfish human beings can be when left free to act on their own," replied the doctor.

"Has this inspection system greatly reduced the number of cases of illness due to tainted food?" The baron asked the question as a way of giving Dr. Doasdo an opportunity to expound the virtues of the arrangement. He did not get the answer he expected.

"No, not at all," the doctor replied. "The number of cases of restaurant food poisoning continues the same as before the law was adopted."

"But then that makes the law doubly silly," exclaimed the princess. "Doesn't it?"

"My dear, you have forgotten the point I was just making in the hall." The sternness had crept into the doctor's tone again. He paused. "About reassurance."

The princess looked puzzled at first, and then brightened. "Oh, I see. You mean that people are reassured by the idea that the government inspectors are looking at the food, whether or not it makes any difference?"

"Precisely!" said the doctor, pleased with the success of his instruction.

We waited 20 minutes longer, tasting the bread and sipping water. Then an elderly official in a tight-fitting brown uniform entered from the kitchen door. "Ah, there's the meat inspector now," said Dr. Doasdo.

The inspector came to our table and tore off tickets from his pad, and placed one beside each plate. Each ticket declared, in rather lengthy language, that the meat had been inspected and declared safe. We noticed that he did not appear to look at the meat at all.

"Now we may begin," said the doctor, "on the meat, that is."

"You mean, there's another inspector for the potatoes?" asked the princess in disbelief. The doctor nodded quietly.

Thereupon, Count Zinn entered the conversation. "Couldn't this inefficiency be easily rectified, Dr. Doasdo? Why could not legislation be drafted that specified that the meat and potatoes be inspected together, by the same person?"

"An excellent suggestion, Count," said the doctor. "And so much in keeping with the spirit of our civilization here in Mandaat! We believe in the continual revision of our laws, so that however badly government works, the belief is maintained that it can always be fixed in the future. I shall put you in touch with a reglamentarian

I know well, Professor Gowidt D'fleau. You can explain your idea to him, so that he may propose it to the Salon in the form of a law."

We began to eat our meat, which, being stone cold, was of course far from appetizing. We noticed that the diners at the other tables had left their seats as soon as they had finished their meat, leaving their potatoes untouched. The doctor suggested we do the same. "I believe the potato inspector is not due to arrive for some time yet," he said in an apologetic tone.

"Oh dear," said the princess. "If this happens every day, I guess we just won't eat potatoes in Mandaat."

Count Zinn interposed, "Don't worry, Princess. Wait for the passage of the Zinn Act!" We laughed politely—although I'm not sure how many of us shared the count's enthusiasm.

Separation of School and State

We passed the early part of the afternoon in our rooms, getting accustomed to our living arrangements. In each room, piled neatly on a side table, we discovered a large bundle of documents. After some preliminaries, I had just settled into reading these materials when I heard a loud thump coming from the princess's chamber. I rushed down the hall to find the baron peering through the open door of the princess's room.

"What has happened?" he asked. "Did someone fall?"

The princess was apparently in a provoked mood and chose not to reply. One of her maids-in-waiting answered the baron.

"She bumped the papers onto the floor, sir, accidentally like."

The stack of documents had been strewn across the floor of the room. "It appears to have been a rather energetic accident," said the baron dryly.

"Silly!" said the princess, spinning around and waving her arms up and down. "Silly, silly, silly, silly, silly!" She stamped her foot. "All these permits. Permits to turn on the water, permits to turn off the water, permits to open the door, permits to close the door. Why, there's even a permit to pick up coins off the floor, if they should happen to fall!"

"Now, Navi," said the baron gently, "I'm sure there's a good reason behind them."

"But, Uncle Koko, nobody knows if we are doing these things. Watch!" She went over to the sink and turned the water tap on and off several times. "See? Who can know if I did it?" She scuffed at the papers with her foot, and then sat down on a footstool. She thought a moment and then said, "Reassurance. That is what Dr. Doasdo would say all these permits are for. But, Uncle Koko, I wonder what is wrong with the Mandaatians that they should need so much reassurance?"

"Perhaps you have a point, Navi," the baron replied, "but still, we had better have the maids pick up these permits and pile them neatly. Since the Mandaatians are so insecure, they are likely to be very touchy about anyone who disrespects their customs."

Later that afternoon, Dr. Doasdo called to take us on a tour of a local church in a two-horse barouche. The avenues were very quiet with practically no one on the street, and hardly any other vehicles to disturb our progress. While we were riding along—we had again been supplied with mandates—the baron questioned the doctor about the church administration. We had been told that the church was a compulsory governmental body, and the baron began the conversation on this point.

"Tell me, Doctor, there are some who say that attendance at religious services ought not to be compulsory, that it ought to be a matter of individual choice and conscience. How do you answer that view?"

"Here in Mandaat, we believe religion is too important to be left to choice. Churches provide the training that enables our people to be responsible citizens. It cannot be left to opinion or chance whether or not some people will get this training. They would end up being deprived of essential tools of successful modern living."

The baron, seeing that the doctor was becoming offended, asked no more questions and we rode in silence the rest of the way.

The church building was a drab structure with a sign identifying it only as "C.S. 104." We noticed that several windows were broken, and slogans—some quite vulgar—had been painted on the walls. We were introduced to the superintendent, a slight, nervous man who held his hands clenched together.

The princess began the interview, pointing to the slogans on the walls. "Why do you have such ugly decorations?" she asked.

"Oh dear, dear, we don't do it. It is done by some of the parishioners who misbehave. They also break the windows, and sometimes even set fires. It's very sad."

"But why do they engage in such deplorable vandalism?"

The superintendent gave a pained expression. "We don't really know," he said, wringing his hands. "Their actions have deep, complex social causes that are rooted in the failings of society. All we can hope to do here is cope."

"Why don't you expel them?" asked the princess.

"Oh dear, oh dear, you can't do that!" the superintendent replied, shaking his head. "Everybody is entitled to religion in Mandaat. And besides, we are forcing them to come. Church truancy is a serious crime in Mandaat. Heavens, being expelled is probably just what they would want. No, coping—and, of course, more funding—that is the only way to handle the situation." The superintendent turned to the baron, "Would you like to see a service?"

He led us down the hall and opened the door of a rather large chamber with a high ceiling. The din was enormous. There were several hundred people inside. Most were conversing with each other, all talking at once; some were eating and throwing litter on the floor; a few were reading newspapers; others were stretched on the floor, apparently sleeping. A heavy pall of cigarette smoke hung over the crowd. The superintendent drew our attention to a woman standing on a platform at the end of the room who was wearing a kind of uniform. Shouting to make himself heard over the noise, he said, "She's reading the sermon." We couldn't hear a word she was saying.

He stepped back into the hall and closed the door to shut out the noise. "We have copies of that sermon, just in case people don't get to hear it. I'll bring you one." He went down the hall and returned with a document, which he handed to the baron.

The baron inspected the document. "At least it talks about God," said the baron, but his face grew troubled as he read more carefully. "Very interesting," he said in that tone he uses when something is amiss. The document was passed around and we saw what had disturbed the baron. The word *God* was there, but no other words with any meaning. For example, the first sentence read:

—the—God—the—and the—.

"What does it mean?" asked the princess. "Where are all the other words?"

"They have been edited out," replied the superintendent. "You see, Princess, our sermons are written by the Board of Sermons, which is under the control of the Salon die Reglement, which speaks, of course, for all the people of Mandaat. Therefore, nothing can be in a sermon that does not meet the approval of all the people. After all, since everyone is being forced to fund religion, that's only fair.

"When religion was nationalized, back in the third epoch, they began with the religious materials they had at the time, and gradually the Board of Sermons eliminated the points objected to by this or that group. For example, that first sentence originally said 'In the beginning, God created the heavens and the earth.' Well, there were some who disputed that God created the heavens, and others who thought God came after the beginning of time, and so forth. As a result of such objections, the passage was edited. In this way," the superintendent said proudly, "we have at last got sermons that serve the needs of the entire community."

There was a long, strained silence. Count Zinn, always eager to put himself forward, spoke. "But is this religion? I mean, what's left? Is it correct to call it religion?"

"That's a highly metaphysical question, sir," replied the superintendent. "All I can say is that the government of Mandaat appropriated 1,262 trillion mandoliers last year for 'religion' and, by jum," the superintendent said with a confident smile, "that's a good enough definition for me!"

With nothing more to be shown at the church, we exchanged pleasantries and took our leave. Although we were careful not to say anything in the presence of Dr. Doasdo, the members of our party were clearly rather shocked at what had become of religion in Mandaat.

On the route back to the Supreme Palace, the princess spotted a handsome building and asked about it. "That is one of our schools, Princess," said the doctor. "Apparently it emphasizes mathematics." The sign on the lawn in front read "Solomon Wise School of Mathematical Excellence."

"May we stop and see it?" asked the princess.

The doctor shifted uneasily. "Strictly speaking, stopping here is not covered in our mandate." He paused a moment. "Let's do this: While you go in to see the school, I will remain here in the carriage, so I can say we haven't really stopped, but have only paused to lubricate the axles. But don't take too long!"

We left the carriage and, our mandates clanking about our knees, walked to the building. At the entrance, we were met by the master, as the director of the school was called. He seemed quite eager to explain the school to us. "We emphasize mathematics here, because mathematics is what will save the world: exact thinking, accurate thinking, honest thinking. So we are rather strict and demanding. Every child commands algebra by age 10, spherical geometry by age 11, and can use and derive from first principles the differential calculus by age 12!" He was beaming with enthusiasm.

"That seems excellent," said the baron cautiously. "But what about the classics? Don't you feel these are important in the education of the young?"

"We teach a little classics, sir, but frankly it's merely an introduction. We can't devote that much time to it if we are to give a thorough grounding in mathematics. Furthermore, classics instructors won't get along with our mathematicians. They want dress codes, for example—which we abhor—and would want to make many other changes. If we included first-rate classics teachers in our faculty, the result would be many compromises and a watering down of the curriculum for everyone. And besides, if parents want their children to study the classics, there are plenty of schools specializing in that; some of them do marvels."

"But if everyone is obliged to fund education through taxes, should not the school offerings be acceptable to everyone? At least," the baron continued, somewhat apologetically, "that's what we were told is the argument for compromising divergent views in the case of religion."

The master raised his eyebrows. "You must indeed be new to this country," he said. "Here in Mandaat, government has nothing to do with education. It's in our constitution: separation of school and state. All our money is raised privately, mainly from attendance fees. Therefore, each school may specialize in whatever beliefs, subjects, and theories the teachers think are valid."

"That is a surprise," said the baron. "But what happens to the poor? If they cannot afford to pay the attendance fees, are they not left without any educational instruction whatsoever?"

"Ah, sir, money is never the problem. You see, we believe in what we do. We want as many qualified children to have mathematical training as possible. If a child comes to us, capable of receiving our training, it pains us to turn that child away. So we devise ways to fund students that cannot afford our training. We set the fees of the other students higher to cover these children; we get them special jobs so they can work to pay part of their fees; and we have a scholarship fund to which graduates and philanthropists contribute."

"This may work here," replied the baron, "but I doubt it could apply in my country. In our duchy, we could not do without state funding of schools."

"Do you really think so? Tell me, sir, do you have state funding of religion in your country?"

"Of course not," declared the baron energetically, the vision of state-funded religion fresh in his mind.

"Does it happen, then, that people are turned away from your churches owing to an inability to pay? Are they excluded from services, or teachings, or listening to the music, on account of their poverty?"

"No," replied the baron with some reluctance. "I see your point. Somehow, other contributors make up the difference."

"And that is exactly what happens here with our schools," the master concluded. "Would you like to see a class?"

He led us down the hall and opened a door. Inside, we could see some 20 boys and girls listening to the teacher in the front of the room. She was speaking about something mathematical that I only partly understood, about "signs" and, I believe, "tangerines." Some of the children, hearing us in the hall, turned to look at us, but the teacher immediately regained their attention, saying, "Eyes front, please."

When the master had closed the door, the princess said, "They seem wonderfully well behaved. And they don't seem to write on the walls either," she added, pointing to the walls of the neatly kept corridor.

"Oh, we insist on discipline here," replied the master. "Without discipline, you cannot teach mathematics, and if you cannot teach mathematics, you cannot save the world. It's that basic!" His eyes gleamed with enthusiasm.

"And besides, everyone here wants to be here. Why shouldn't they listen carefully to their teachers?"

As we returned down the hall, the baron spoke. "On this question of voluntary schooling, what do you say to the argument that education is too important to be left to choice or accident? Don't schools provide the training that enables people to be responsible citizens? Shouldn't everyone be required to go to school?"

"What a horrible thought, forcing people to go to school!" The master shuddered. "Why, imagine what this school would turn into if our students were driven here by soldiers and policemen! It would be almost as bad as a church!"

We thanked the master for his explanations and excused ourselves, citing the problem with the mandates as the cause of our hasty departure.

"I understand," said the master, with a sympathetic glance at the placards dangling at our knees. "After all, mandates are what we pay for civilization." His right eye seemed to wink at that moment, which made it uncertain if he was sincere in saying this.

Once in the carriage with Dr. Doasdo again, the baron commented, "I find it somewhat surprising that the government here in Mandaat does not control education."

"But Baron," replied the doctor, "this is a part of our constitution: separation of school and state. Mandaat is a free country, after all!"

"So we were given to understand," said the baron.

There was silence for a time as the horses went clip-clopping down the avenue. Then the doctor spoke again. "Of course, I agree that private education, being unregulated, is open to many abuses. It is not very reassuring to think that, in education, people may do anything they like."

He paused, staring thoughtfully out the window. "Not reassuring at all."

The Hideout of the Nibblelaries

As I had anticipated, it was too much to expect that the princess, with her impulsive nature, would remain clear of trouble for the entire visit. Although, in fairness, she was hardly to blame for the crisis that befell in Mandaat.

Our rooms in the Supreme Palace were on the first floor on the east side. They faced a block of tenement houses where some Mandaatian families lived across a rather narrow street. On the afternoon after our visit to the church and school, the princess was sitting at the window of her room, idly watching the houses across the way. She was exceedingly bored, for nothing was planned on our tour, and the mandate regulations had of course restricted her from even venturing outside for a walk.

Gazing upon the houses opposite, the princess spotted a child, a 3- or 4-year-old girl, sitting in an open window, playing with a doll. She waved at this child, who smiled with delight and began to wave back at the princess in a most vigorous fashion. In the act of waving, however, the child let the doll slip, and it tumbled down to the street!

The princess scarcely hesitated. She saw the child was beginning to cry over losing the doll, a loss that the princess herself had, indirectly, caused. She ran down to the door at the street and looked out. Glancing up and down, seeing no sign of commissioners, she assumed that she could cross without detection. She rushed across the street, retrieved the doll, and handed it back to the child in the window.

At just that moment, she heard a shrill, crow-like honking. Alas, a commissioner had been lurking in a doorway at the far end of the street! "Caw! Caw! Caw!" went his horn as he rushed up the street toward the princess. Perhaps this noise frightened the princess, or perhaps she had reached some kind of breaking point with all the restrictions of Mandaat. Whatever the reason, she was unwilling to allow the officer to apprehend her. Instead, she turned and fled down the street!

In response, the commissioner's horn changed pitch to a shriller, louder tone. Apparently, this was a signal to other commissioners in the vicinity to join the chase after a mandate evader. Almost immediately, the princess was being pursued by an entire band of commissioners in their little black suits, all honking their horns, like a flock of angry crows chasing a sparrow.

The noise terrified the princess, who ran faster and faster down the street, then around a corner, then up another street and around another corner. This burst of speed put her ahead of the commissioners for a moment. Unfortunately, her shipboard life had left her in an unexercised condition, and she had to stop for lack of breath. The shrill caw-cawing began to draw closer, but she could hardly move her feet. Then she heard a sound from a nearby doorway.

"Psst! Psst!" A young man was waving at her to enter. She had little choice if she were to escape her pursuers. She stepped inside and the young man quickly closed the door behind her.

"Oh, thank you!" she said, haltingly gasping out each word. As she looked at the lad, she saw that he was handsome and well formed, but was wearing tattered clothes. His hair was also rather long and not well combed.

"My pleasure," he replied with a warm smile. "Come upstairs and meet the boys."

He led the princess up two long flights of stairs—she had to pause several times to catch her breath—to a small third-story room where a number of boys were seated on the floor. He invited her to sit on the floor, and then called out, "Cora! We have another evader! Bring something for her to drink!"

Then he turned to the princess. "This," he signaled toward the group of a dozen boys seated on the floor, "is the Amac-Amic Underground Group." The boys smiled at her in welcome. One stood up and shook her hand.

"We are one of dozens of such secret societies, people who challenge the mandate laws and act to assist others, like yourself, who are being pursued by the commissioners. We believe that the mandate laws, like all the laws of Mandaat, are immoral. It is our goal to undermine this regime!"

"I certainly want to thank you for saving me from those men," replied the princess. "I don't know what would have happened to me without your help." She nodded to the group. "And I agree that the mandate laws for the use of the streets seem most silly and unfair, as are just about all the other laws here that I've seen."

At that moment, an older woman hobbled into the room carrying a steaming mug. She had a warm, kindly face and welcomed the princess with a broad smile. "This is Cora," said the young man with a wave toward her, "and my name is Rebbie."

The princess took the mug and tasted the drink, which was called "lotz." It was not unlike hot cider, except that it had a stronger taste and, as the princess was to discover, a stronger effect!

Sipping her drink, surrounded by the friendly fellows her age, the princess felt safe and content. They asked her many questions

about Pancratica, which she was pleased to answer. Then she asked them about their group and its purposes. She learned that its name had been taken from that of an ancient chief of the Liberta tribe.

"When are you planning to start your revolution, Rebbie?" asked the princess.

"Why, never," he replied. "You see, we don't believe in revolution."

"That is a surprise. I thought all revolutionaries believe in revolution."

"Ah, but we're not revolutionaries. We don't believe in trying to knock over the regime by force. As all history shows, all that brings is the new use of force by the revolutionaries once they are victorious. They set up a new government that makes more laws enforced by more policemen and commissioners, and pretty soon you're back to where you started.

"No, Princess," he continued, "we are not revolutionaries. We are nibblelaries! We nibble at the laws, so as to make them harder and harder to enforce. We evade them, just enough not to get caught, or we stretch them to confound their original intent. That is how we challenge the mandate laws. We dart across streets, and then run away, too quickly for the commissioners to be able to catch us. As more and more people join us, the laws will simply become unenforceable!"

"I see," said the princess. "And when this regime is overthrown—"

"Undermined," corrected Rebbie.

"—Undermined, I mean . . . what will you replace it with?"

"Nothing!" responded Rebbie. "No rules, no regulations, no laws, no anything. Then everybody will be able to do as they please."

"But won't there be chaos?"

Rebbie smiled and a few of the boys giggled. "I see you've been listening to the reglamentarians' propaganda." He paused to choose his words. "What's chaos? What do you mean by 'chaos'?"

The princess thought a moment. "Does it mean people dying?"

"But people die in Mandaat every day," replied Rebbie. "The Salon die Reglement doesn't stop that."

"Maybe it means people bumping into each other?" ventured the princess.

Rebbie smiled. "Do you realize that as a result of the mandate laws, we have built tunnels and corridors under the city so people can get around? They are full of people walking back and forth. The Salon doesn't do a thing about it, because they know if they regulated halls and tunnels, we'd all starve!"

"Then maybe chaos means people being unhappy?" suggested the princess.

"And the Salon has prevented unhappiness in Mandaat?" asked Rebbie, throwing his arms apart. The boys smiled at his theatrics.

"No," he continued, "'chaos' has nothing to do with the actual daily lives of Mandaatians. It refers to the illusion of control. Each person in the government seeks to force others to do his will. That's what a person means when he speaks of 'chaos.' He means that people are not doing what he wants them to do."

The princess suddenly realized she was becoming extremely sleepy. Something about the lotz was making her mind slip. There was another question she wanted to ask Rebbie, but she could not seem to pull it from her brain. "But what about . . . ?" That was all she said before she fell into a deep, quiet slumber.

—*w*—

Meanwhile, back at the palace, the baron had to grapple with the difficulty caused by the princess's disappearance. Of course, the maids had seen her flight from the commissioners. The baron decided that to avoid scandal and possibly something worse, it was best to keep her lawbreaking from the authorities.

At supper that evening, Dr. Doasdo inquired about the princess. The baron declared her to be ill, thinking this a plausible excuse, but he failed to reckon with the thoroughness of this highly regulated society.

"I'm afraid," said the doctor, somewhat apologetically, "in that case, she must have a sickness permit."

The baron pursed his lips and tried to appear unconcerned. "Is that so?"

"Yes, I'm afraid it is. She must be inspected by a physician—for she might have something contagious, you see."

"My, my," said the baron, "you do indeed have many regulations here in Mandaat!"

"Yes, Baron, and notice how they reinforce each other. It's like a giant spider web. Each regulation gives us an opportunity to detect lawbreaking of another kind. Of course, that wouldn't apply in this case."

"Of course not," replied the baron, shaking his head vigorously.

The physician-inspector arrived at our quarters later that evening, and it seemed inevitable that the princess's absence would then be discovered. But the baron surprised us with his stratagem!

He first told the physician that no doctor could be allowed to see the princess because the laws of Pancratica forbade the princess to be immodestly exposed.

The physician granted the point—he was most sympathetic when it came to legal requirements—but continued to insist that he could not give a permit without seeing the princess.

"Tell me, Doctor," asked the baron, "must you see all of the princess? Surely you don't inspect every square inch, even the soles of the feet, and so on?" The physician admitted it was true, that he did not need to see all of a patient to give a permit.

"Then I believe we can arrange a compromise," said the baron. He led the physician to the princess's boudoir. He rapped upon the door, "Princess, we are ready for the examination."

The door opened just a crack, and a delicate, feminine hand was extended (the hand, of course, of one of the maids). "Here, Doctor," said the baron, grandly waving his hand at the exposed fingers, "is the part of the princess you are duly authorized to examine!"

The medical man accepted this declaration, made his examination of the hand, signed the permit, and left! In this way, we were able to keep news of the princess's disappearance from the officials of Mandaat.

———

Meanwhile, in Rebbie's hideout, the princess was having a long sleep. When she awoke, the sun was streaming through the windows and the room was empty. She found that a blanket had been put over her. She sat upright. "Hello?" she called out.

Cora came clumping in from the adjoining room. "Good morn', dearie—or . . . it's nearly 'good afternoon,' that is, for you've slept 'most half a day!"

"It must have been the lotz," said the princess, shaking her head to clear her dizziness. "It was stronger than I thought." Then she remembered her position. "Oh my goodness, I must get back to the palace! How can I do that?"

"Don't worry about a thing," said Cora patiently. "Rebbie and the boys'll fix it. They know how to do such things. But first let me get you a breakfast, for you must be famished!"

Cora brought a plate of scrambled eggs and fried carrots, which had to be placed on the floor, as there were no tables—or any other furniture—in the room. The princess, sitting cross-legged on the floor, found the meal no less tasty than the most elegant feast ever served in the castle at Plotz.

"Tell me, Cora," she asked when she had finished, "do you believe that Mandaat can really do without its government and all its laws?"

"Ay, who could say?" replied the woman. "All I know is that if everyone is like my dear boys, then no, it never could work."

"What do you mean?"

"Because they're not even able to take care of themselves, not to say others. Who cooks here? Who picks up here? You should have seen this room after they left last night: paper, food, mugs all over. I pick it all up. Don't take me wrong. I love my boys like sons, and I don't mind doin' for 'em." She collected the breakfast things and removed them to the kitchen.

When she returned, she said, "Oh, they're good at sneaking around and foiling the commissioners. But I say, how are the streets going to be clean? The streets are clean now, because the government does it. When there's no government and just my boys running up and down, do you think the streets are going to be clean?"

"I think I see what you mean," said the princess thoughtfully.

Shortly afterward, Rebbie entered with two of the boys. "Ah, Sleeping Beauty is awake," he said with mock grandness, "and desires to be wafted back to her castle." The princess smiled.

After thanking Cora for the breakfast, she joined Rebbie and the boys, and followed them down the stairs to the basement. There he led the party into a small, low tunnel that had been roughly hacked out of the earth. Soon, this tunnel connected to a larger passage that was full of people walking rapidly back and forth. "See, Princess, this is how we Mandaatians get around."

"They don't seem to be bumping into each other, particularly," said the princess.

Rebbie gave a conspiratorial wink. He led her along the main corridor for several blocks and then turned up a flight of stairs. "Here we must cross the street, for the tunnel does not run in this direction. We will wait for the decoys to clear the way." The boys went out first. Their assignment was to draw the commissioners away, by running down the street in opposite directions. The sound of caw-cawing soon reached their ears.

"Quick!" said Rebbie. "Across the street!"

They dashed across the street, down a stairway and into another tunnel, where they joined a crowd of people. Walking along the corridor for several more blocks, they came to a door. "This is the stairway up to the palace, Princess. Here is where I say goodbye."

"Oh, well then, thank you." She said. "Thank you so much!" Then the princess gave Rebbie a quick hug, turned, and pushed open the door.

She entered and quietly shut the door behind her. Before her was a highly ornamented spiral staircase made of iron. Gathering the folds of her dress with one hand, she began to tiptoe up the steps. She had gone about halfway when the door at the top opened and an official came clanking down the stairs in his big leather boots. The princess, unsure of her position, turned around and began descending. The official spotted her.

"Stop there!" he called out as he came clumping down the stairs. "What do you think you are doing?"

Though he was eager to catch her in the wrong, he obviously did not yet know what transgression the princess had committed. She saw a chance to trick him. "I was intending to leave the palace," she said.

"Do you have a palace-leaving permit?" he asked.

"Well, no, not exactly," she replied.

"Then you cannot leave," he said sternly. "You must go back and get a palace-leaving permit—and, of course, a palace-returning permit to be able to come back in."

"I'm terribly sorry," said the princess. With a nice display of reluctance in her step, she climbed the stairs, while the official glared at her from below, to see that she followed his order.

She went through the door at the top into the corridor, breathless and triumphant at having outwitted this official of Mandaat. Adopting a firm, authoritative manner, so that no official might challenge her, she walked briskly along the passages—making a few wrong turnings in the process—until she at last arrived at the door of her chambers.

She was greeted with great joy by her maids-in-waiting. The baron was, of course, relieved and delighted at her safe return, though he made a show of scolding her for her impetuous behavior. The princess bubbled with high spirits as she recounted her adventures. I fear she was rather exhilarated at having successfully defied the bureaucracy of Mandaat. "I've become a little bit of a nibblelary," she said with a laugh.

There is little more to tell of our visit to Mandaat, for we left the afternoon following the princess's return. However, an episode of note occurred at the final luncheon at the Supreme Palace. We had been served our meat and potatoes and were waiting, as usual, for the meat inspector. When this gentleman finally appeared, he surprised us by not coming to the tables. Instead, he took a position by the wall.

"Why aren't you inspecting the meat?" Dr. Doasdo called to him.

The man came over to our table. "Because, as of today, new regulations have relieved me of this job. Someone recently made a suggestion, and the nincompoops up above"—he jerked his thumb in the direction of the Salon die Reglement—"have decided that the potato inspector is also given the duty of inspecting the meat."

At this point, we remembered the proposal to improve the inspections. Everyone looked at Count Zinn, who made himself small and stared intently into the water glass he held between his hands.

The meat inspector continued, "Because that inspector is inspecting sawdust at the mill, he won't be here for several hours.

"That's why nothing ever works in Mandaat," he went on, "because they have idiots making the laws. If they would just get intelligent, sincere people as reglamentarians, they could fix all these problems."

Our meal that day consisted of bread and water only.

—∿—

Several days later, at supper on the *Giovanni*, we were discussing the government of Mandaat and trying to explain how it grew into its present oppressive form.

"What puzzles me," said the baron, "is that the regime is quite without any theory or guiding ideology. Each measure is approved simply out of a desire to improve things, to make things safer, or"— the baron nodded toward the princess with a smile—"to reassure the public. Yet the result is a state more rigid and dictatorial than one governed by religious zealots."

I added: "If Mandaat has any official ideology, it is probably the ancient philosophy of freedom of the Liberta ancestors who are so venerated in the Salon die Reglement. Yet that philosophy is wholly transgressed in practice even while lip service is paid to it."

"I would assert," said Count Zinn in a pompous tone, "the real problem is that Mandaat does not have enough sincere public officials."

The princess countered him immediately. "How can you be so silly, Count? The idea of having a single inspector at the restaurant was your idea, and you were sincere. Yet that left us without any lunch at all!" The count lowered his head in embarrassment. "No," she continued, turning back to the rest of the party, "it's not the sincerity of the reglamentarians. The problem with Mandaat is that it has too many laws, too many for anyone to manage properly."

She turned to the baron, "How many laws is the right number for a country to have?"

The baron gave a pained expression. "Mandaat did indeed have too many," he replied thoughtfully.

"But if reducing the number of laws makes a country better," the princess continued, "couldn't you keep going? I mean, make the country better and better by having fewer and fewer laws? Until you'd end up with no laws at all!"

"How unrealistic you are, Navi," replied the baron. "You have to have laws. Otherwise, there'd be no point in having a government."

"But do you have to have a government? Rebbie doesn't think you have to have a government."

"Accept what I'm saying, Navi, that's all toffle-boffle. It's inconceivable to have a country without a government."

At that point in our travels, we had no grounds for questioning the baron's declaration.

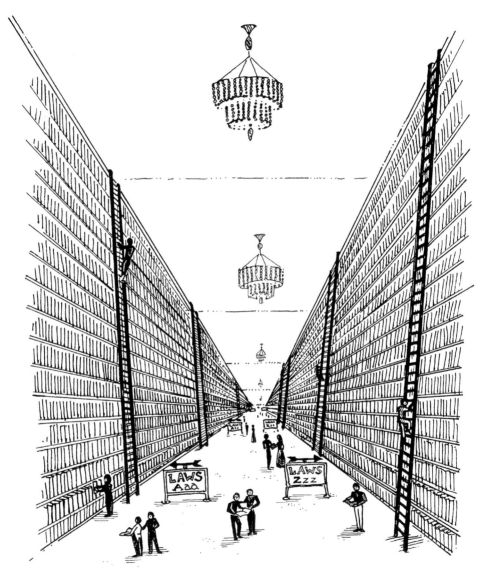

Mandaat's Hall of Laws

Princess Navina Visits
Nueva Malvolia

On the eighty-first day of our tour, the baron called the princess into the mizzen cabin of the *Giovanni* and announced that preparations had been made to visit our next country.

"What is it to be, Uncle Koko?" asked the princess, discretely shifting the book she had been reading out of sight behind her back. "I certainly hope it isn't another 'M' country, like Malvolia or Mandaat with their horrible laws." She rolled her eyes. "I've become rather fatigued with 'M' countries."

The baron smiled at her playacting. "Well, it isn't an 'M' country." He hesitated, then added, "At least, not exactly."

The princess stiffened and looked at him with alarm. "What do you mean, 'not exactly'?"

"My dear, the country is called Nueva Malvolia."

The princess eyed the baron suspiciously. "Does it have anything to do with Malvolia?"

"Well, er, it is a former colony of Malvolia. But," he added hastily, "now it is completely independent and much more modern. It is even said to be a democracy."

"But do the rulers still have the idea of being mean and horrid to their subjects?"

"Well, yes, unfortunately, they still maintain their philosophy of serving, as they say, the greatest misery for the greatest number."

"But, Uncle Koko, you know what happened before. I made complaint of this creed, and the magog almost imprisoned us. Surely we should not put ourselves in such danger again!"

"Have no fear, my dear," replied the baron. "Nueva Malvolia is completely different on that score. They observe complete freedom of expression." The baron took up a parchment from his desk. "As my correspondent reports, 'Everyone incessantly condemns the government, yet all walk in complete liberty.' So you see, Navi, we shall be completely safe, no matter how much you criticize the rulers."

"I wonder," said the princess thoughtfully, "whether anyone can be safe in a land where rulers seek the unhappiness of their subjects."

Our arrival in Nueva Malvolia was marked by a disconcerting episode. Our vessel had been tied up and we disembarked to wait upon the quay for officials to arrive. Suddenly, we heard a cry and a feminine voice wailing, "Oh my, not again!" Down the street, a young woman was being surrounded by a gang of toughs wielding wooden clubs studded with bent nails and exposed staples. Naturally, the Pancreatic regal guard, led by our indomitable Harry Hotspur, rushed to the aid of the damsel and surrounded her attackers with drawn swords.

Strangely, the attackers did not relent. The leader of the villains turned boldly toward our men, and undertook to order them, saying, "Cease and desist in the name of the law." This official language, and the authority with which it was uttered, gave pause to our swordsmen. We noticed that the members of the attacking band were all wearing the same gray and black-checked capes and pantaloons: They were apparently in some kind of official uniform.

Count Harry persisted. "Unhand that woman," he said, waving his sword at their leader's nose.

"Calm yourself, fool," said the leader of the band. "We act on state authority. Disperse before you end up in magistrate's court."

Count Harry, angry at the insult, but confused, looked inquiringly at the young woman, who had long, flowing dark hair and sparkling black eyes.

"Alas, he is right," she said. "I can see you are strangers here and don't understand our ways. This is what we call a mobbery, and it's quite legal." She handed her purse to the assailants, who took most, but apparently not all, of the money in it and handed it back. The assailants then departed, leaving the woman with her bewildered would-be rescuers.

"Don't be too disappointed," she said, laying her hand gently on Count Harry's arm. "It was very kind of you to want to help."

"I still don't understand," he said, shaking his head.

"Those were the men of the government," she said. "They roam the streets and accost people at random, taking money from their purses and wallets."

The baron entered the conversation, "But why do you have such a gross custom?"

"It is hideous, isn't it?" she replied, wrinkling her nose. "But then, what can one do? The poor babes would have such cold feet if it weren't done. Mobbery, after all, is the price we pay for civilization."

This remark left us more puzzled than ever, but we were unable to satisfy our curiosity further, for at just that moment we were interrupted by a clatter of horses drawing three opulent carriages. These contained the delegation that was to escort us to the palace. This group included the ruler, who introduced himself as the paterog of Nueva Malvolia.

The paterog was a tall, husky man with a rather attractive face. He was modestly dressed in a brown suit, and proved to be a friendly fellow, eager to make himself liked—a welcome contrast to the haughtiness of the magog of Malvolia.

When we had settled ourselves in the first carriage, the baron mentioned that we had visited old Malvolia and met that ruler.

"Ah yes, dear Uncle Horace," he replied with an indulgent smile. "So earnest, yet so old-fashioned. Always making himself out to be so cruel and hard-hearted."

"Then you seek to appeal to your subjects?" asked the princess.

"But, of course," replied the paterog. "I have to have the approval of the people in order to win elections."

"We have heard about your elections here in Nueva Malvolia, and have come to study your regime on that account," said the baron.

The princess frowned in puzzlement. "But if you have elections, and seek to be liked by your subjects," she said, "then surely you don't pursue the policy of making your people miserable, do you?" She paused. "For if you did, then everyone would hate you and not vote for you."

"You're mistaken there, my dear," replied the paterog amiably. "There is no compromising our basic, historic creed. I seek the misery of the people just as keenly as Uncle Horace does. We just go about it more intelligently here." He winked and regarded our group with a broad smile.

After enjoying our stares of curiosity for a few moments, he explained himself. "The key to an enduring policy of misery is to cause the public to believe that the harmful policies are necessary for their own good! That way, they view the rulers who carry out these policies as their benefactors!" The paterog was beaming with enthusiasm.

"I don't see how that could be possible," said the princess. "To inflict injury on people, yet make them desire the injury and praise you for inflicting it?"

"We do it all the time," replied the paterog. He glanced back down the street where the young woman was standing, clutching

her purse in dejection. "I understand you witnessed
just now?"

"We did, indeed," interposed Count Harry, still smarting from
the episode. "What is the meaning of that vicious practice? It seems
nothing but outright robbery!"

The paterog smiled. "It would be robbery, Count, if you did it:
most reprehensible. But when I do it, it's mobbery, and the people
approve of it."

"We have seen that is the case," said Count Harry, recalling
the young woman's endorsement of the practice. "But how can
you justify it?"

"On the basis of intentions, sir. Good intentions. Here in
Nueva Malvolia, we defend each of our hurtful policies in terms
of some good intention that it is supposed to serve. In the case of
mobbery, the funds are used to pay for public pedification."

"I beg your pardon?" asked the count. "I have never heard
that word."

"That is our program of providing free footwear for everyone
in the country, especially for the poorest children. Without it,
as I continually remind the public, the waifs would go unshod,
and suffer dreadfully. So"—he gave a broad smile—"here's an
example of a harmful policy that the people have been trained
to accept because it has a worthy aim." The paterog rubbed his
hands together.

"There's one thing wrong with your case," said Count Harry,
who was growing increasingly irritated. "It is ruinous to commerce.
Because everyone fears being attacked by your reeves, they take
only small amounts of money with them when they go out on the
street, and therefore they can't buy things they want, and trade suffers in consequence."

"Exactly so, Count. That's the beauty of mobbery," he said. "In addition to being splendidly vexing, it has the side benefit of trammeling manufacture and trade." Count Harry glowered.

The princess tried to take up his case. "But don't the people object to mobbery on account of this harmful side effect?"

"Have no fear on that account. That's the beauty of politics, of regulating things from afar. The public doesn't see how our meddling causes harm. Scholars write at length of the indirect evil effects of my policies, but no one ever buys their books. Here, good intentions trump analysis."

This conversation left us confused and dejected. Shocking as it seemed, the paterog had apparently developed a viable system for promoting misery.

On the walk up to the palace, a small incident occurred that, because of its later significance, needs to be noted. New Tension, the capital of Nueva Malvolia, proved to be a dirty, trash-ridden city, with garbage in the gutters, vile slogans painted on walls, and wastepaper blowing about. One of these papers came to rest in front of our party as we approached the main portal. The princess, reflecting her fine breeding, stooped to pick it up.

"You shouldn't do that," said the paterog. His demeanor, which up to this moment had been genial, was surprisingly tense.

"Why ever not?" replied the princess.

"Just because," was all he said. The princess decided to ignore him, and deposited the paper in a nearby dustbin. The paterog scowled, but the matter was soon forgotten, and he again took up his charming chatter.

We entered the Palacio Central and were escorted to the Indian Treaty Room, a majestic reception hall whose walls were decorated with fine inlaid mahogany. Waiters in livery served us a local beverage, a brown, sparkling liquid called Aloc-aloc, which tasted rather appealing. When asked what it contained, the paterog told us it contained no vitamins, minerals, or nutrients of any kind, but only additives designed to be harmful to health. "It fits perfectly with our philosophy here," he said, smiling broadly. We drank rather less of the stuff after we heard this.

Baron Kolshic began to question the paterog about political practices. "Tell us, sir, which of the policies of old Malvolia apply here? Do you have, for example, negamos?"

"Oh yes, indeed. The idea of giving regular payments to anyone needy or distressed is, of course, an important method of promoting neediness and distress. But we have gone far beyond this. Negamos drag down only one category of citizens, those who are less motivated or less capable. Our more energetic and determined citizens are not affected by them."

"Do you not have prosperity fines, as they do in Malvolia?" asked the baron. "I mean, the system of imposing progressively greater monetary penalties on those who earn greater amounts of income?"

"Yes, we have those too," replied the paterog. "Unfortunately, the prosperity fine demoralizes only those workers motivated by material gain. Many energetic and creative people have higher motives. They want to improve the world, or make discoveries, or demonstrate their ideas. Taking money away from them is insufficient to destroy their ambition and render them apathetic."

With some reluctance, the baron asked the obvious question. "How, then, do you subvert these more idealistic individuals?"

"I meddle!" The paterog gave a broad smile.

"I beg your pardon?"

"I meddle. I enter into each and every activity and introduce laws and regulations that make it impossible for inspired and energetic people to carry out their projects."

"That seems shockingly vile," said the princess. When the paterog only chuckled, she went on, "But surely everyone is outraged by this policy. Doesn't it ruin your popularity?"

The paterog obviously enjoyed the question. "Ah, my dear, you have forgotten my strategy of good intentions. When I meddle, I don't say my goal is to destroy the idealism of creative people. I tell them that I intervene in the name of some good cause. There's practically no institution you can't ruin by forcing people to obey good intentions imposed from afar."

The paterog took no notice of our disapproval, and continued. "Why, just last week, I destroyed a boys' club in one brilliant stroke. What did they call it, Manny?" He looked to one of his aides.

"Men of Madison, sir."

"Yes, Men of Madison. Well, this club was taking troubled young boys, giving them pride and a purpose, getting them engaged in constructive activities. And other clubs were starting to copy their methods. I said, 'Whoa there! Can't have youths not turning into juvenile delinquents.' So I passed a law requiring all boys' clubs to admit girls, saying that it was cruel and unfair to exclude girls from such a successful program. It was beautiful! The volunteer who founded and directed the club resigned in anger, most of the boys didn't want to change the name, so they dropped out, and no girls could be persuaded to join anyway. So the club is utterly wrecked!" He slapped his thigh with delight.

Harry Hotspur could contain himself no longer. Since his unsuccessful effort to stop the mobbery in the morning, he had been fuming all day. "You are a low knave, indeed," he said with the thick Scots burr that enters his speech when he grows angry. "If I denounce you, sir, will you give me satisfaction?"

The baron gasped. "Sir Harry, remember yourself! There will be no dueling!" He turned to the paterog. "I must apologize for the heat of my subordinate."

"Think nothing of it," he replied, genial as ever. The paterog turned to Count Harry. "Denounce away, young man, only there shall be no duels or reprisals. Here in Nueva Malvolia we have complete liberty of expression."

Count Harry clenched his fists.

"I see the baron is looking at his watch," continued the paterog, "and that it is time for you to repair to your quarters." He turned and motioned toward the doors of the Treaty Room. "My assistant will take you." He indicated an attentive young man dressed in a neat blue suit standing to one side. His full name, we found out later, was Emmanuel Pulate.

Turning to this young man, he said, "I believe they have rooms reserved at the Inn Trapment, Manny." Turning back to us, he said, "We've just installed Occurama service in every suite there." He smiled and gave us a wink.

At the time, I supposed this was some arrangement for delivering meals to guests, and I looked forward to seeing it in operation. I should have paid more attention to the name of the hotel.

An Enthralling Device

"You see, I was correct," said the baron as we entered our hotel suite, and he handed his cane and gloves to the steward. "There is no danger in criticizing rulers in Nueva Malvolia. They do believe in freedom of expression. Hello, what's this?" He had spotted, as we all had, a great glass globe in the middle of the room, supported at eye level by an elaborate metal structure.

"That is an Occurama, sir," replied Mr. Pulate. "It's an entertainment device. Would you like me to turn it on?"

"By all means," said the baron. "We merit some relaxation on this journey."

Pulate went to the wall and pulled down on a large lever. A gentle rumbling was heard underneath the floor. We looked at the glass globe, and saw a most wondrous sight. Within the globe, a mass of colored liquid began to move and heave, forming and reforming itself into exciting patterns of color and light.

"How beautiful!" exclaimed the princess. "How does it work?"

"It's driven by horsepower. Here, look." Pulate pointed out the window. Next to the building we could see a horse walking on a treadmill. Tubes and pulleys ran from this structure into our building, and apparently connected to the Occurama under the floor. "Every day," continued Pulate, "the Occurama has to be recharged with new pigments, brought by the purveyors."

Everyone watched in silence, captivated by the swirling colors in the globe. "This," said Pulate, "is one of the government's most ingenious programs. It is our aim to have an Occurama in every home within five years."

"But why should the government have an interest in this device?" asked Count Harry. "It seems a pleasant enough toy, hardly capable of harming anyone."

Mr. Pulate grinned and winked. "The paterog said it would be all right to tell you, as visitors, the theory behind our policies, so I can explain the Occurama to you."

"You mean it is intended to cause unhappiness?" asked the princess.

"Oh, yes indeed," he replied. "The idea for it grew out of a custom they had in old Malvolia, of putting people in prison as a way of making them unhappy. The principle was quite sound, of course, as far as it went. The human organism needs challenge and activity. If you compel people to be idle, and seal them off from the demands and opportunities of life, you can lower their morale and self-esteem, and make them, in fact, unhappy. Jail does do this. But its action is not complete, because it does not occupy the mind. In jail, people can still read books, write letters, and think independent thoughts.

"Jail has a second disadvantage: It is unpopular. Once we began using elections in this country, we saw that we would have to end the practice of imprisoning people for no reason. So we began to look for something people would like that would deaden their minds and draw them into wasteful inactivity. Occurama is the result of this search."

"And do people actually watch it?" asked the princess.

"Oh, indeed they do," replied Mr. Pulate. "Most of their waking hours. And here"—Pulate pointed to a row of tiny push buttons at the front of the Occurama—"you can see our latest innovation. You push these buttons to help change the colors and patterns in the globe. It creates a psychokinetic attachment for the user that is positively addicting!" He turned to the baron, and waved him toward the machine. "You're welcome to try it, sir."

The baron came up to the machine and pressed one of the buttons. The color of one sector of the globe instantly changed from yellow to magenta. The baron gave a chuckle of delight. He pressed another button. A streak of silver passed across the base of the globe. The baron gave a little gasp of excitement.

Pulate continued with his lecture. "Now our laboratories are working on a Super-Occurama that will have moving pictures.

When that is perfected, newscasters will appear on the screen emphasizing the many risks and dangers in the world, in this way multiplying the public's anxiety and dismay."

Pulate's account of the Occurama produced a confusion in our thinking. We were delighted to watch the pulsating globe—the baron couldn't seem to stop pressing the buttons—but now that we understood its evil purpose, our pleasure was tainted with guilt.

Count Harry was the first to speak. "We should turn it off! As the young man says, it is designed to degrade us."

"I'm afraid that's not possible," said Pulate. "The Occurama is so constructed that once you turn it on, it cannot be turned off."

"Then we must leave this room," said Harry, turning to us.

"Count Harry is right," said the princess. "Let us go to our chambers, and when we meet for our tour this afternoon, let us avoid this room and meet in the hall."

As we filed out, we noticed the baron remained in front of the machine, pushing at the buttons with great rapidity, his fingers flying like a dressmaker's. "Uncle Koko, aren't you coming?" asked the princess with some alarm in her voice.

"I think I'll stay here and experiment with this for a few minutes," he replied. "It has certain educational aspects." The princess frowned, but said no more.

Later, after we had refreshed ourselves in our rooms, Mr. Pulate took our party on a tour of the city—all except the baron, who remained at the inn playing with the Occurama.

One of the first things we noticed as we walked the streets was a number of decayed murals. The paintings must have been beautiful at one time, but they had been sorely neglected. The paint was peeling, and vandals had scrawled slogans over them. Pulate overheard us commenting upon their sorry state.

"Yes, they add nicely to the sense of decay and hopelessness, don't they? That is the result of one of my own initiatives."

He said this with pride and anticipation. I thought it a good opportunity to snub the man by saying nothing, but our Count Zinn, who cannot bear a silence unfilled with the sound of his own voice, rushed in. "And how, pray, did you achieve that?"

"Not too many years ago, building owners began commissioning artwork on the walls. This was most undesirable: It made the city look cheerful and interesting, and gave artists work to do and the joy of self-expression. What could we do about this? The first impulse would be to ban murals—but that would have made us appear uncivilized. No, the proper strategy was meddling." His face broke into a broad smile.

"The idea I came up with was an act for the Protection of Art. We said that artwork is so precious and so sublime that it is wrong ever to alter or destroy it." He mimicked a speechmaking tone, waving his arm toward the sky in a grand gesture: "We must respect the creative genius of our artists, and cherish their creations!"

"A most noble idea," said Count Zinn, duped by his discourse. "That's the kind of policy we should have in Pancratica." He imitated Pulate, waving at the sky. "Art first, I always say."

Mr. Pulate smiled, assuming that the count was joining his sarcasm, and continued with his explanation. "It meant that if a painting deteriorated, no one could touch it. It also meant that no building with artwork could ever be torn down, repaired, or altered. Very quickly, owners declined to have any artwork on their buildings, and the whole joyful industry of decoration and mural painting has been squelched." He smiled and gave Count Zinn a knowing nudge. "As our teenagers would say, we roasted the roach!" Count Zinn smiled uneasily in confusion. I couldn't help musing, not for the first time, that if the poor count would think before he spoke, he would be spared much embarrassment.

At just that moment, three unruly youngsters ran through our group. One slapped Count Harry on the back of his head and another pulled the princess's hat to the ground. Count Harry drew his sword, but the boys ran away quickly.

"Another fruit of our policies," said Mr. Pulate, gesturing at the fleeing boys.

"You mean you actually promote juvenile delinquency?" asked Count Harry, seething with anger.

"Oh yes, Count. We have numerous policies to ensure that our children remain idle, ignorant, and undisciplined. It's the easiest thing in the world to do. Whenever we add a regulation to hinder healthy processes of nurture, discipline, or growth, we simply say"—he again adopted a speechmaking posture and mimicked a maudlin tone—"it's *to protect the children.*

"For example, it used to be that many youngsters worked in shops and businesses. This kept them busy, taught them skills and responsibilities, and gave them feelings of self-worth. So, of course, we had to put a stop to it. We said children were being exploited, that they were exposed to dangers and hardships. To protect the children, we said, child labor must be outlawed.

"The policy works beautifully," he continued. "Now children spend their time watching Occurama—which makes them morose and even suicidal—or they hang about the streets drinking Alocaloc, and engage in vandalism—which is, of course, more dangerous than work would ever be!"

"And does no one object to your policies of undermining youth?" asked the princess.

"Not when you cloak it in good intentions. There's almost no policy, no matter how destructive, that people won't accept if it has an apparently good purpose. Here's an example of a success we had just last week. In the town of Fairfield, in the shire of Califo, there was an after-school care center run by a woman who had no arms. She gave a shining example of overcoming disability. Everyone marveled at what she could do with her chin, her body, and her feet. She loved the children and the children loved her. For 20 years, she provided high-quality care without a complaint from anyone.

"*Whoa there!* we said, here's just too much happiness, too much positive energy, to allow. Of course, we couldn't close the nursery outright. That would make us look cruel and heartless. We needed to meddle with a well-intentioned regulation. Unfortunately, this woman kept complying with each one that we devised, but finally, we hit on one that defeated her: We said all child care workers must be certified in CPR—the heart attack treatment where you push with your hands on the child's chest. Well that roasted the roach! So now her care center is closed, and the children remain alone at home—with Occurama, and matches, and other lovely things—and no CPR either!"

"But surely," said the princess, "people pointed out how silly the CPR regulation was, that children hardly ever have heart attacks, and that CPR would almost never be used to save a life even if they did?"

"When they did, we trumped them with good intentions. We said that even if one child in a million might be saved by the regulation, it would be worth it." He adopted a tone of mock anger and shook a hectoring finger at the princess. "How, madam, can you in good conscience oppose a law *to protect the children?*" He made his voice quiver on this last phrase.

"The secret, you see," he said, his voice returning to normal, "is to focus on the good intention of the policy, to make the public keep its gaze on that shining hill, so that it never notices all the evil effects of the legislation."

We made no comment, but Mr. Pulate went on, caught up in the enthusiasm of his narration. "Would you like me to explain the measures we have adopted to hinder and degrade the education of our youth?"

Members of our group looked at each other with dismay. After a few moments of silence, the princess spoke, in a weary tone. "I think we have had enough for one day."

Salvation by Trash Collection

When we returned to the Inn Trapment, we found a most worrisome situation. The baron was still playing at the Occurama, seemingly unable to take his eyes off it. But he was unwilling to recognize his peril. "Oh, come now," he replied when Count Harry tried to remind him of the evil purpose of the device. "How could a toy like this do any harm?" His speech was slurred and dull, and his face remained expressionless as he gaped at the machine.

The next morning, this "toy" precipitated a crisis. Our plan had been to say our farewells to the paterog at the Palacio, and to go from thence to the *Giovanni* and depart. But as we prepared to leave the inn, we discovered that the baron wished to remain. He had, in fact, spent the entire night watching the Occurama, and was fully captured by the device—indeed, addicted! "We need to stay here a few more days," he said dully, his eyes riveted to the glass globe, "in order to make sure we understand everything about the country."

The princess tried to reason with him. "Uncle Koko, you're not paying any attention to the country. You're sitting here all the time!" When the baron made no reply, she continued, more insistently, "It's time to leave! You said another destination is already arranged. Where is it?"

"Voluntaria," said the baron in a flat tone, still not taking his eyes off the globe.

"Well, then, we must depart." The baron took no notice. "Uncle Koko, please!" She grabbed his hand and tried to pull him up from the couch, but his weight resisted her effort. It was clear that he would not leave of his own free will.

In the side lounge, we held a conference. "We'll just have to pull the man away from that vile machine and drag him to the boat," said Count Harry, "kicking and screaming, if that be the only way."

"Count, you forget yourself!" said Count Zinn. "The baron is the commander of this expedition. He is your military superior, and mine too." Count Zinn wagged his finger at Harry. "It would be mutiny for us to force him against his will!"

Harry glowered at Count Zinn, but he knew he spoke rightly. "Aye, you've a point there," replied Harry, biting the words off through clenched teeth. "We can't do the dragging. But that's the only way to save the baron's besotted soul." To our looks of shock at his strong words, he added, boldly glaring back at us, "With all due respect."

"Perhaps," said the princess, speaking slowly with her brows furrowed, "perhaps we could get the paterog to command a brigade of police to move the baron to the ship?"

I felt the possibility was unlikely, because it was based on the assumption that the paterog would want to relieve our distress, a distress deliberately caused by one of his engines of misery. But it was not my place to question the princess's proposal.

We made our way to the Palacio and were eventually admitted to the paterog's office. After he heard the princess's proposal, he rose from his desk, smiling and laughing.

"Deport someone for watching Occurama? Heaven forbid!" Then he said, in a more serious tone, "The only time we would deport a visitor is when they threaten our values."

When no one said anything, he added, "Frankly, I think the best solution is for the rest of you to start watching Occurama and enjoy it." He gave the princess a wink.

"When hogs fly!" said Count Harry hotly, who turned on his heel and strode out. After some hesitation, the rest of us followed.

Back at the inn, we discussed strategy. At first glance, we seemed to be in an impossible situation, destined never to be able to leave Nueva Malvolia.

"Count Nef," asked the princess, turning to me, "how can we make the paterog put the baron on the ship? Is there not some diplomatic folderol to get put out of a country, persona au gratin, or something like that?"

"There is," I replied. "We could have our party declared *personae non gratae*, that is, persons undesirable to the regime."

"That's it!" she exclaimed, her eyes lighting up. "The paterog said he would deport us if we threatened the principles on which Nueva Malvolia is based. So perhaps that would be the answer."

"Aye," said Count Harry bitterly. "Except that this infernal country is based on wrongdoing, and that monster is offended by nothing, neither criticism nor injury. In this topsy-turvy land, if we burned down half the city, he would like us all the more."

"Then we must try goodness," said the princess.

"I beg your pardon?"

"That's it, Count!" the princess continued, her eyes glowing with excitement. "Since the paterog loves wrong and all that leads to unhappiness, it's logical that he despises that which contributes to the people's well-being. The way to have ourselves declared persona whatever-it-is and deported is to engage in something beneficial!"

"But what shall that be?" asked Count Harry.

The princess's brow furrowed. We looked around at each other with enquiring eyes.

"I know," the princess said suddenly. "Remember how upset the paterog got when I picked up that paper blowing in the street? There's a good deed that will upset him. Picking up trash from the streets of New Tension!"

The idea was so apt that we lost no time putting it into effect. Our entire party—except the baron, of course—went out to the street, and we began a plan of collecting the wastepaper into barrels we obtained from the inn. It was hard work, but by noon, we had rendered a three-block stretch entirely clear of trash and looking quite attractive.

During our labors, many passersby stopped to observe and comment on our project. They thought it commendable that we were improving the appearance of the city, but they also found our behavior perplexing. "The government is supposed to do that," they said.

When we began work again after lunch, a number of the local youths spontaneously joined our efforts. At first we were apprehensive, recalling their rudeness of the previous day, but we found them most congenial and eager to please. As to their motives, I suspected that they wanted to challenge the regime because they sensed, perhaps unconsciously, that it was the source of their wretchedness.

Whatever the reason, by the end of the day, several dozen boys and girls were working alongside us, and with their help, we had cleared 14 blocks—an entire neighborhood, in fact.

On the following day, the number of youths aiding our efforts rose to more than 100, and we cleared 56 blocks. Many government officials were observing our activities and making careful jottings in their notepads, so we knew the paterog would not ignore us much longer.

We had underestimated his cunning, however. On the next day, as we were beginning work along Scream Boulevard—a major thoroughfare of the city—an official arrived to read a proclamation. A considerable crowd gathered, including the boys and girls and many adults who had come to watch our unusual labors.

The official unrolled a parchment and began to read in a stentorian voice: "The gathering of trash by minor children is hereby prohibited, pursuant to section 301F of the Health and Welfare Act of the Realm."

A tall man standing in the crowd spoke up. "But that doesn't make any sense! The children are doing something useful and constructive. Why are you outlawing it? Isn't this a free country?"

"Ah, but you see," said the official with a patient tone, "gathering trash is dangerous. The children might pick up items with harmful infectious bacteria, which could make them sick—or even start an epidemic. Or they could cut themselves on something sharp. Why, four years ago, a child in Tyburg cut herself on a piece of glass. The cut became infected and they had to amputate her arm. So you see what can happen."

A sigh of sympathy passed through the crowd. "How dreadful!" said the questioner shaking his head. "Well, we certainly don't want anyone to lose an arm. We must think of the children."

Provoked by the crowd's easy acceptance of the paterog's propaganda, Count Harry rushed up to dispute the man.

"That's ridiculous!" he said, shaking his finger in the man's face. "You've accepted a false argument. Why, the world is full of dangers and harms. If you keep trying to legislate against them, you will end up with a police state that paralyzes all growth and achievement! Don't you see?" He looked around at the crowd. "The paterog is tricking you with his strategy of good intentions."

The tall man drew back. "Well, I don't know, really, one way or the other," he said quietly. He shifted uneasily, seeking some way to escape from the confrontation with Count Harry. "I think we have to trust the experts. Government wouldn't do these things if it weren't for the best." Count Harry clenched and unclenched his fists but said no more.

This new development brought our activities to a standstill. The paterog had used against us his nefarious tactic of meddling, and it seemed we were defeated. The youngsters gathered around, awaiting some direction.

The princess's face was stern and there was fire in her eyes. She waited until the official disappeared around the corner. Then she whispered, with an intensity I had not seen in her before, "We shall become nibblelaries!"

The youths murmured in anticipation. Of course, they did not understand the meaning of her declaration, for they knew nothing of the princess's experiences in Mandaat, but they could clearly sense from her manner that she meant to resist.

"We shall keep picking up trash," she continued, addressing the youths, "but only when officials aren't looking. We'll post lookouts to warn us when inspectors come, so that you can pretend to be wasting your time in bad and idle activity when they come to check."

The boys and girls were elated with her idea. "That'll roast the roach! Yo!" they shouted, raising fists and spin-jumping in the air. They arranged their lookouts, who were given whistles of ear-splitting intensity, and soon they were back at work, picking up the litter with redoubled energy.

Those of us in the royal party from Pancratica were uneasy, however. Count Zinn voiced the thought many of us had in mind. "Princess, aren't you advocating evading the law? Is that proper?"

The princess bit her lip and thought a moment. "Count," she said in a firm, deliberate tone, "when you're dealing with deranged government, evasion is the only moral response."

After pondering the matter myself, I found it hard to fault her logic.

The nibblelary strategy proved to be a success. Every time the paterog sent officials to check up on the activities of our delegation, they found youngsters idling in the street, pushing and shoving each other, uttering curse words, and playing a dangerous local knife game called "Stab the Slowpoke." Of course, the youths were only pretending to be engaged in this vicious pastime, but the inspectors took it as real and reported that all was well and that all laws were being fulfilled.

However, the city was becoming cleaner day by day, and everyone knew that we were doing it. Even the newspapers remarked upon it. One editorial, in particular, seemed to be the straw that broke the camel's back. It said, "We owe a debt of gratitude to these aliens with their miraculous powers. In cleaning up the city, they are accomplishing in days what the government has failed for decades to achieve."

The morning after that editorial appeared, we were out working on Vile Street when officials swooped down upon us from all sides, pushed us into coaches, and drove us directly to the harbor. Before anyone had hardly drawn a breath, we were on board the *Giovanni*. We found the baron and all our baggage from the inn already on board.

The paterog was standing on the quay beside the ship—I think he wanted to verify with his own eyes our certain departure. Count Zinn made a feeble effort to protest that our treatment was a violation of diplomatic protocol, but everyone on both sides understood that our departure was mutually convenient.

As the lines were being cast off, the paterog addressed us. "Of course I had to stop you. If my subjects ever realize that they can do for themselves what my government claims to do for them, it will be the end of my regime." He lifted his hat. "You made an extraordinary effort, I'll give you credit." We smiled in triumph.

"What on earth was that all about?" asked the baron as the ship headed out to sea. "I was minding my own business, quietly playing at the Occurama when officers kicked down the door— kicked it down!—and carried me off to the ship. Just like that. It was most disconcerting, I can tell you!" He looked around at us. "Do you have any idea why?"

Worried glances flashed back and forth among the members of our party. Because we had acted to subvert his desire to remain with the Occurama, it did not seem prudent to explain to the baron the true circumstances of our departure. I had to think fast.

"Well, sir," I said, "the object of the paterog's regime is to disconcert people, so I expect this was just one of his random acts of unpleasantness that we have learned so much about."

"Of course, that's the explanation, Count. How perceptive you are!"

—♦—

That evening after supper, we discussed the regime of Nueva Malvolia. "If there's one thing I'm learning on this trip," declared the princess, "it is to beware good intentions."

"Well, they certainly are the source of much unhappiness in the world," Count Zinn ventured to say.

"But are good intentions always harmful? Is it wrong to want to help people? Is it futile to try to make the world a better place?"

A long silence followed her remark. Was the young princess becoming a cynic already? I began to wonder if this world tour was a good idea for her after all. Fortunately, Count Harry knew how to respond to her query.

"It's all a question of distance," he said. "Good intentions bring good results when you're close to what you're doing, so you can know the effects of your actions. Suppose you were trying to cook a meal from far away, so far away that you couldn't see it, or smell it, or taste it. Suppose you were up on the poop deck using the speaking

tube to tell a seaman in the galley how to make a pudding, telling him when to add salt, when to remove the pudding from the oven. Would the dish turn out well?"

The princess hesitated, and Count Harry went on. "Of course it wouldn't, because you're too far away from what you're doing. You might say 'add salt' when it already had enough salt."

"I see your point," said the princess slowly. "You can't cook a meal from a distance."

"But," Harry continued, "that doesn't mean one can't ever cook anything successfully. It just means you have to be close to what you're doing to make your good intentions come out well."

"I think I see," said the princess. "What's wrong with politics is that everyone's trying to fix things from a distance, like cooks trying to bake a pudding through the speaking tube. No wonder they blunder. When you tend things right under your hands, you can succeed." She paused. "Just as we did"—she lowered her voice and turned slightly away from the baron—"in our little you-know-what project on Scream Boulevard." She smiled, and Harry winked in reply.

The princess needn't have worried about the baron catching on, for he wasn't following the conversation. In fact, he'd had a rather dazed, inattentive air about him all evening. "I wonder," he said, speaking to no one in particular, "if they make a miniature Occurama? Wouldn't it be jolly if they made a portable one, one small enough to take aboard a ship, let us say?"

The company received this remark with stunned silence. The princess rolled her eyes in a most charming way, but kept her peace. I think she is growing up.

Princess Navina Visits
Voluntaria

"My, isn't this grand!"

Baron Kolshic was referring to the reception, complete with a band whose brass instruments sparkled in the sunshine, that awaited us on the pier in Voluntaria. As our vessel drew near, we could make out signs saying, "Welcome to Voluntaria," and many people waving little colored flags.

This was a great improvement over the unpleasant arrivals in the other countries. In Malvolia, we had been set upon by rude and aggressive beggars. In Mandaat, we had been denied the use of the streets by an obnoxious petty official, and in Nueva Malvolia, we were forced to witness a deplorable, but legally permitted, robbery. These distasteful experiences had sorely tried the baron's dignity, and he was therefore elated to encounter a welcome in Voluntaria that reflected credit upon him and the Pancreatic delegation.

Swelling with confidence, he turned to the princess and gestured toward the crowd, saying, "Here at last, Navi, we have found a country with a proper, excellent government for you to study!" This comment lodged in our memories because, as we were to discover, it was so thoroughly mistaken.

As we stepped onto the pier, a tall woman dressed in a pink gingham gown and a blue bonnet came forward to greet us. She introduced herself as Mrs. Gloria Reade, and explained she was in charge of the welcoming party. The group also included her son, Philippe, a lad of about ten years, who played trumpet in the band. After exchanging greetings, she spoke of the arrangements for our lodging, which seemed most unusual. We were to be boarded in the private homes of members of the welcoming party. "You, Baron, and the princess, will be staying in our home, if that suits?"

Of course the baron did not refuse such a hospitable offer.

As we made our way through the streets of Refugio—this is the name of Voluntaria's port city—we noticed that everything was clean and carefully kept, with flowers adorning practically every dooryard. When we remarked on the attractiveness of the houses, our hostess laughed good-naturedly. "Oh, that's the eagerness for ratings."

"Pray, what ratings are these?" asked the baron.

"Three different groups make them," she replied. "The most important is the Garden Association. Each year, the RGA publishes a ranking of all the neighborhoods, rating each one according to its beauty and appeal. The neighborhoods vie hotly to be high on the list. It's not just pride, either. There's money involved." She nodded knowingly. "They say being in one of the top neighborhoods adds 4,000 mintos to the price of a house. Imagine that! As far as I'm concerned, every neighborhood is practically as good as any other, but there you are."

We soon arrived at the Reades' home, a house as beautiful and well cared for as any in Refugio. There we met Mrs. Reade's husband, Nathan, a stocky man with a nearly bald pate. He wore tiny pince-nez glasses that gave him the appearance of owlish wisdom. He explained that he was by trade a printer and bookseller, but was largely retired and now devoted most of his time to community projects. We were told that Genna, their 18-year-old daughter—almost the same age as our princess—would arrive later from her school.

After unpacking and refreshing ourselves, we met with the Reades in the study, joined by other members of our party staying in other homes. Mr. Reade began by asking us what we wished to see during our stay.

"Studying your government is, of course, our main purpose," said the baron. "We were hoping you could direct us to it."

"I don't believe I recognize that word," replied Mr. Reade, "and I'm well versed in vocabulary, being in the printing trade. Philippe," he said, turning to his son, "would you kindly see if you can find the word in our dictionary?"

The boy went to the large volume on the table and leafed through the pages. "No, the word doesn't appear." He bent over the book and slowly ran his finger down the entries. "The listing goes from 'gopher' to 'gown' with nothing in between."

"That's ridiculous," said Count Zinn. "Why, every country has a government."

"Yes, it's most unusual," said the baron. "Undoubtedly, what has happened is that here in Voluntaria, 'government' is called by some other name. For example, Mrs. Reade," he said, turning to her, "I assume your welcoming committee is part of the government. If you tell us who your superiors are, who directs you and who pays your salaries, then that agency, whatever it is called, is the government of Voluntaria."

"But no one directs us," she replied. "We are simply an association of people who are proud of our country and want visitors to have a pleasant stay and carry away a good report of our society."

"Then how did you find out we were coming? How did you know when to meet us?" asked the baron. "I wrote a letter addressed to the director of protocol of the government of Voluntaria."

"From that letter, Baron. It was given to us by Postmistress Barney. When she gets letters from abroad with no known address, she turns them over to us in case they are from travelers seeking information." After a pause, Mrs. Reade added, "As for money, we are, of course, funded by voluntary donations." She glanced around at our group. "By the way, you don't happen to have any leftover currency from other lands that you would like to donate to our Voluntaria Cosmopolitan Society?"

"Remarkable," murmured the baron. Then, realizing she had asked a question, he said, "Yes, I believe we may." Everyone in our group turned out his pockets, and soon there was an avalanche of malotes, mals, and mandoliers, so much currency that Mrs. Reade, blushing with pleasure, had to fetch a little basket to hold it all.

"Thank you so much, everyone," she said. "Now, after we take this to the exchangers, we'll be able to afford a tuba for our band!"

When the hubbub had died down, Count Zinn returned to the previous subject. "The welcoming group may not be governmental, but that still leaves us with the job of finding the government here, called by whatever name it has. For Voluntaria must have one."

"Not necessarily!" These words came from Count Harry Hotspur, and we knew that a dispute was in the making, for Count Harry and Count Zinn are like oil and water, never agreeing about anything. "I don't think we should go making assumptions before we have the evidence," said Harry. "They may well have no government at all here in Voluntaria."

"Yes," added the princess. "Remember, in Mandaat, Rebbie said that you didn't need to have a government. Well, maybe that's happened here."

"Nonsense, nonsense," replied Count Zinn. "I'll bet my portion of butter treacle for the rest of the voyage that we find the equivalent of a government here in Voluntaria." This was no light offer, for butter treacle was the most highly prized dessert on our ship.

Count Harry pounced on the challenge. "I accept your wager, sir! I declare that we shall not find a government here in Voluntaria."

They sealed the bet in the traditional Pancreatic way, by banging their knuckles together—rather more forcefully than the custom demanded—and glaring at each other.

"Gentlemen, gentlemen!" said the baron. "What impression of Pancratica must we be giving our hosts! Please forgive their excess of spirit," he said, turning to Mrs. Reade.

"Think nothing of it," she replied. "A good debate tills the mind, as we say." She smiled indulgently at the sparring men. Turning back to the baron, she asked, "But how, indeed, shall you decide your question?"

"The method of proceeding, it seems," said the baron, "is to start with those tasks carried out by our government back in Pancratica. This will lead us to what is, in fact, the government of Voluntaria. One good place to start would be the streets and public works, which are everywhere a government responsibility. Who," he asked, turning to Mr. Reade, "owns your streets and who takes care of them?"

"The streets, Baron, are owned by individual property holders," said Mr. Reade. "For example, I own the section of street that runs in front of this house."

"But that would mean that a street would be owned by hundreds of people!"

"That's correct."

"But how could it possibly work? Why, each owner could deny access to his part of the street, could he not?"

"Well, he could, and this does occur in very rare cases. But consider what is likely to happen. If, I, for example, should deny access to the portion of the street in front of my house, the property owners on either side could deny me access to the segments of the street that they own. It would therefore be impossible for me to leave or enter my house! I would very quickly learn the advantage of cooperating with my neighbors. As we say here, either we catch the lion together, or it eats us singly."

"Yes, I see your point," said the baron. "But surely, some restriction on the use of the streets is necessary. To prevent certain types of vehicles from using them—like wagons with spiked wheels that would break the paving stones, for example?"

"Naturally," replied Mr. Reade. "That is the job of the neighborhood associations. Every part of the city has a grouping of the property owners in that area. In Refugio"—he turned to the bookshelf, removed a volume, and opened it—"there are 38 neighborhood associations. This book contains all the information about them; you're welcome to study it at your leisure, Baron," he said, handing the book to the baron. "The neighborhood associations act as agents for property owners. They decide about maintenance, and getting firms to do snow removal, and they also set the rules for the streets in their area.

"For example, one of the most vexing problems we have is dealing with motors, these new gasoline-powered carriages they've developed recently. People object to them because they're noisy and smelly, but they're useful to move heavy furniture and make deliveries. A few associations still ban them altogether, but most have adopted the practice of allowing them on the streets from 10 a.m. until noon. Tomorrow morning, Baron, at ten o'clock, you will see a dramatic change in the character of our streets. That's when the work of the town gets done."

Count Zinn asked a question. "How do you raise money for these neighborhood associations?"

"Why, through voluntary donations, of course," replied Mr. Reade. "Just this morning I sent our association a check for

100 mintos to put up hanging flower baskets. It's all voluntary donations—is there any other way?"

There was a pause, as the count hesitated to answer what seemed so obvious a question. Finally he spoke. "In Pancratica, we use taxation."

"I don't believe I've ever heard that word either," said Mr. Reade. Looks of bemusement passed among the members of our party.

"Well," said the count, "it's a system where the government asks people for money."

"Then it's the same as here," said Mr. Reade, "because our neighborhood associations, indeed all our associations of every kind, ask people for money."

The baron entered the conversation. "Ah, but what happens if people choose not to give it?"

Mr. Reade looked perplexed. "Nothing, nothing at all," he replied.

"Well, there's the difference. You see, with taxation as we have it in Pancratica, you're forced to give up the money. If you don't, we put you in jail!"

Mr. and Mrs. Reade looked at each other in alarm.

"Perhaps we are not understanding you," said Mr. Reade with measured politeness. "You ask a person for money, he declines to give, so you lay hands on him and drag him away?"

"Yes."

"And what if he resists?"

"Then the agents would subdue him."

"Strike him with a club, for example?"

"Well, we wouldn't like to see that, but, yes, it might come to that. No one must be permitted to contradict the authority of the government tax collectors."

Mr. and Mrs. Reade again exchanged significant glances. To end the awkward pause, Mrs. Reade said, "We have heard about that in, what was the country? Nueva Mandaat, or somewhere? They have a custom called mobbery."

"Oh, it's nothing like that," said the baron emphatically. "Mobbery is an arbitrary seizure of funds. Taxation, as we practice it in Pancratica, is governed by regulations. The rules say how much money each person in each situation is forced to pay to the government."

"But it seems to me," said Mr. Reade, "that to cover all the different situations that must arise, these rules would have to be very extensive, would they not?"

"Oh, indeed. There are over 15,000 pages of regulations."

"And to apply and enforce all these regulations, you would need hundreds of clerks and agents, would you not?"

"Actually, it takes scores of thousands," said the baron with some pride. "In fact, our Pancreatic Intensive Revenue Service has 107,000 employees this year."

"Why, that's practically an army!" exclaimed Mr. Reade, shaking his head in disbelief. "Wouldn't the people of the country fear this agency, and resent it? And wouldn't they always be trying to cheat it?"

"Well, there's quite a bit of that," answered the baron. "That's why we put people in jail, to try to stop the cheating. Last year, we sent more than 2,500 people to prison for disobeying the tax authority."

"It seems incredible," said Mr. Reade, "that such a barbaric system could exist. But if you say it does, then I must accept your testimony." He paused and looked at Mrs. Reade. "It just goes to show how adaptable human beings are. If people are determined enough, they can make any social arrangement work, even a highly offensive and burdensome one."

"But, sir," said the baron, somewhat nettled by Mr. Reade's patronizing observation, "how else can you possibly raise funds for public services? Why, one must compel people to give. They won't contribute just out of wanting to help the community. It's against human nature."

"Well then, Baron," said Mr. Reade, "you and your colleagues must not belong to the human race, for just a few moments ago, I witnessed you giving Mrs. Reade donations to the VCS!"

The baron looked confused. "Well, that's different. Very different." He paused. "The . . . the welcome society is an activity we approve of—we can see its value. Naturally, we want to support it. Taxation is necessary to support activities when people don't want to support them."

Philippe spoke up. "But—begging your pardon, sir—why do something people don't believe in?"

"Because, because . . ." The baron looked around the room for assistance. "Count Zinn, perhaps you can explain it to the boy."

"Yes, er, well," the count said loudly but with uncertainty in his voice. He paused and pressed his fingertips together and began to speak. "There are certain things, certain services, which a decent society must have, but which the people, being selfish, are unwilling to support."

"Begging your pardon, sir, but, like what?" asked Philippe.

"Well, er, like parks, for example."

The boy looked at his father in puzzlement. "We have those in abundance," said Mr. Reade. "Some are donated by wealthy citizens; others have been created by voluntary associations for special purposes. In fact, you can see one of them from this window." He walked over to the window and pointed. "There, at the end of the street. That's a sculpture garden operated by the Clevelle Society."

Count Zinn frowned. "But, just a moment," he said. "Some people may contribute to the common good under your voluntary system, but surely not everybody does so? That's the point of taxation: to force everyone to contribute."

"You are correct," replied Mr. Reade. "There are always some who don't donate for one reason or another. For example, I'm pretty sure our next-door neighbor, Mr. Flint, did not contribute to the hanging baskets." Mr. Reade gave a hearty chuckle. "He would probably say the baskets weren't quite right in some respect or another, but we all know he just likes to watch his pennies. If I were collecting money for some good cause, he would not be the first I would approach." Mrs. Reade and Philippe joined him in laughing at what was obviously an understatement.

"Doesn't this make you angry?" replied Count Zinn. "Here you are, helping to make the town look beautiful, and your stingy neighbor does nothing. Don't you want to force him to contribute to the public good?"

"But if I did that, Count, I would be acting out of resentment," replied Mr. Reade. "Surely you're not saying that resentment is a sound basis for public policy?"

An awkward pause ensued, and Mrs. Reade wisely turned the conversation into other channels. "Customs differ, of course, and everyone's right in his own way, isn't that so, Baron?" Rushing on, she asked, "So, tell us, what are your plans for tomorrow?"

"Well," the baron replied, "we still face the problem of finding the equivalent of government here in Voluntaria."

"If there is one," Harry quickly put in.

The baron ignored the remark and continued. "In most places, education is a task of government, so perhaps we should look to this field. I think it very likely that we shall find that the agency behind education here, called by whatever name, is the government."

"If it's education you are interested in," said Mr. Reade, "then our daughter Genna is the one to show you about all that. She's preparing herself as a teacher, you see, and I'm sure she would be happy to take you to her school tomorrow."

"I'd love to see it," said the princess.

"Another thing government does," said the baron, "is care for the poor and needy. Mr. Reade, is there any agency that does this here in Voluntaria?"

"Oh, indeed, there are dozens. Perhaps the most important is a group known as Craftmasters. I'm sure they'd be happy to have you visit them."

"Very well," said the baron. "Count Zinn, why don't you and Count Harry pursue that subject tomorrow?" The men exchanged wary glances, then nodded in acceptance of the assignment. "The princess will look into education, and, for my part, I will see who really is behind the streets and public works. One way or another, we are going to find a government in Voluntaria!"

The Curious History of Voluntaria

The next day, we were all busy with our investigations and making ourselves familiar with Refugio. This city of nearly half a million inhabitants is built up from the shore and extends up into steep hills overlooking the sea, with many of the houses practically perched on cliffs. As we walked along the streets, we noticed many small shops, but saw little sign of large companies or large trading centers. We saw almost no commercial advertising, and many of the shops even lacked signs to identify themselves. Evidently, customers knew the businesses they patronized very well.

A number of large billboards, however, carried messages to influence manners and public opinion. For example, one of these—of great interest to our party after our misadventure in Nueva Malvolia—had a picture of an overcooked fried egg with this caption:

This is your brain after Occurama!

Another, which I did not understand until some days later, showed a picture of an attractive young woman in a bathing suit. It said,

Swim in the Neckar?
The Nature League will make it possible!

At the bottom, it directed donations to a particular address.

Perhaps the most unusual thing we noted in our first steps around Refugio was the friendliness and helpfulness of the inhabitants. I found that if I but paused to get my bearings, people would inquire if I needed assistance or directions. Once, while I was standing at a corner making some jottings in my diary, my street map slipped from my grasp. Almost before it had reached the ground, a man had retrieved it for me.

At supper that evening, we remarked on this general atmosphere of friendliness, and asked our hosts how they might explain it.

"Well," said Mrs. Reade, "as we say here, 'Courtesy is the mother of civilization.' We teach it to all our children from a very early age. 'Courtesy is the mother of civilization and generosity is the father.'"

"In Pancratica, we teach that courtesy is important, too," said the baron, "but with much less effect. We have many rude and self-centered individuals, I'm sorry to say."

"Perhaps," said Mr. Reade, "this is because your society does not really depend upon courtesy."

"I beg your pardon," said the baron. "I don't understand your point."

"Apparently in your country, as Count Zinn was explaining to me just before supper, you use prisons, and whipping posts, and fines to punish misbehavior of every kind, is that not so?"

The baron nodded.

"Therefore, it would appear that, as revealed by your actual practices, you believe that civilization depends on force, not upon courtesy." An awkward pause followed this remark.

"Well, perhaps that's true in a sense," said the baron, finally breaking the silence. "But surely you, too, believe in using force. How can you direct society without it?"

Mr. Reade pressed his palms upon the tablecloth. "I think that perhaps it's time to give you some background about the history of Voluntaria." He took a sip of water.

"Here in Voluntaria, we are extremely reluctant to employ any use of force. I am speaking of physical force—hitting, piercing, holding a human being against his will, physically destroying his property by smashing it, burning it, and so on. In our scale of values, violence—physical violence—is the greatest evil." He paused to let the point sink in.

"It was not always so," he continued. "Voluntaria was at one time an extremely violent country."

"Yes, the Apple Wars!" This interruption came from Genna, the daughter who was becoming a schoolteacher.

She put her hand over her mouth. "Oh, pardon me, father."

"That's quite all right, dear. Go ahead and tell them about the Apple Wars."

"Many, many years ago," said Genna, "Voluntaria was torn by warfare between two factions, known as the Reds and the Whites. These battles, which went on for centuries, were known as the period of the Apple Wars."

"Why on earth were they called that?" asked the princess.

"From the way they cut fruit. These groups differed in their method of serving fruit. The Whites cut apples lengthwise, and the Reds cut them across." Her brow furrowed and she looked at her father. "Or was it the other way around? I always get it mixed up."

Philippe parroted, "Reds spread, Whites bite."

"Of course, I forgot." She nodded at the boy. "Thank you, Philippe. The Reds cut lengthwise. Of course, this isn't why they fought such terrible wars. In fact, no one can figure out why they fought so much—but they did, seizing each other's lands and crops, burning villages, and so on. Horrible atrocities were committed. Our history books tell about the massacre at Jeraco, for example, where the Reds massacred the entire population when they captured the city! Some time later, in what's known as the Slaughter of the Poppies in the region of Anway, 70 percent of the population was slain in battles and massacres!"

"How horrible!" exclaimed the princess.

"Of course it was, and people finally got sick of it. Some of these people called themselves voluntarists. They believed, as Daddy says, that violence is the worst of all evils. Their leader was Herbert Herbert. He said that you shouldn't use force for anything, well, or almost . . . ?" She gave a puzzled look at her father.

"Yes, that's nearly correct, dear. Actually, Herbert was the leader of what we now call the 'perfection' wave of voluntarists. The first, or 'founding,' voluntarists were absolute pacifists. They said that force was totally evil, that you shouldn't use it at all. They formed communities of like-minded people, but they made no effort to defend themselves because they didn't believe in using force. Each group prospered for a time—until one of the marauding bands came and pillaged them. Such episodes seemed to teach everybody the lesson that nonviolence is a foolish, unrealistic ideal. Then, after another generation or two of warfare, the idea of nonviolence would revive, and new pacifist communities would form, only to be devastated by raiders again.

"It was Herbert Herbert who had the vision for advancing beyond this dreadful, perpetual cycle. He agreed with the founding voluntarists that force in general was evil, but went on to declare that the greatest evil was the initiation of force—in other words, striking the first blow, firing the first arrow, breaking into a house, and so on. Therefore, he said, in order to defeat the greater evil of a violent attack, it was permissible to use force for self-defense." Mr. Reade paused for a sip of water.

"Well, as I said, this perfected the philosophy of voluntarism, and made it a basis for a durable society. Voluntarists withdrew into communities of like-minded believers, but this time fully prepared to defend themselves with force. The first of these communities was Citadel, founded by Herbert himself, and our oldest city." He nodded to the princess. "It's really a lovely city, by the way. You must see it if you have time on your visit."

"And it's got the largest steam engine in the country pumping its water!" Philippe added.

"Yes, indeed," said Mr. Reade, smiling indulgently at the boy.

He continued his story. "Following that lead, other communities started, adopting the principle of trying to avoid the use of force, but being willing to use it against those who initiated force. These communities were successful and prosperous, and gradually extended their scope, while the bands of warriors and robbers gradually disappeared. Finally, our land came entirely under the sway of these voluntarist communities, as it is today."

This account so amazed us that we hardly knew what questions to ask. The baron began cautiously. "In some respects, your history is very much like our own, for we, too, have seen much futile bloodshed, and one wonders why people didn't see the senselessness of it." The baron turned to me. "You're the historian, Count Nef. Why didn't we in Pancratica develop an opposition to violence? Why didn't we have a Herbert Herbert teaching us that the initiation of force was the greatest evil?"

"We did have such people," I replied. "But they were considered dreamers and cranks. That's why no one has ever heard of them."

We proceeded to enjoy the meal that Mrs. Reade and Philippe had prepared for us, a stew called "chularoo," which they said was a traditional dish in this land. It is made of vegetables that neighbors have donated to each other from their gardens, so that its composition varies somewhat according to the season. After we had finished the course and the plates had been cleared away, the baron spoke. "Well, now, has anyone succeeded in discovering the equivalent of government in Voluntaria? Princess, did you find a government in charge of education?"

"I don't know anything about that," she said, "but I can say that what Genna is doing in her school is remarkable! She has this system of teaching children to read by using colors and music, and a big stand-up doll she calls Mr. Kaboo. The children put the letter blocks in this hole in his stomach—it's difficult to describe. You'd have to see it to understand how it works. Even her smallest children are reading like professors!"

Mrs. Reade spoke up. "Did she tell you she is going to open a school of her own next year?"

"Yes," replied the princess. "Isn't that wonderful? I would love to stay here and teach in her school!"

The baron asked Genna, "And where did you go to get a permit to open this school? I ask the question," he said, turning to the rest of the table, "because it may enable us to solve our problem. It is almost certainly the government that authorizes new schools." He turned expectantly back to Genna.

"I didn't get permission from anybody. I'm just going to do it. Daddy and several other friends have agreed to provide funds. And I have a list of six teachers from my school who have agreed to be endorsers—because it always helps in promoting a new school to say established teachers approve of you."

"Well, then, how about licensing?" continued the baron. "Who gave you a license to teach?"

Genna looked puzzled and glanced to her father for help.

"What do you mean by a 'license,' Baron?" asked Mr. Reade.

"It's a piece of paper that the government gives you saying you are allowed to do something, in this case, to teach in a school."

"No, there is nothing like that here," said Mr. Reade. "Genna can teach anyone, anywhere, and no one can stop her."

This seemed so contrary to practices in Pancratica that the baron was tempted to question further. But in the interest of avoiding another disagreement, he changed the subject. "Yes, well, be that as it may. . . . Now, Count Harry and Count Zinn," he said, turning to those gentlemen, "did you succeed in finding a government agency taking care of the poor?"

Count Zinn hung his head and was silent, but Count Harry was eager to answer. "No, sir, we did not. The group called Craftmasters is a voluntary organization supported by voluntary donations."

"And what does it do, Harry?" asked the princess.

"It provides food to the destitute by having them earn it working at tasks they can accomplish. You should see the workshops," he said turning to the baron. "There are rooms and rooms of different activities. They even have one workshop where blind people are crafting sculptures, and these sculptures, I understand, sell for a very high price."

"Indeed, they do," said Mr. Reade. "These sculptors are among the leading artists of the city."

"That's all very well," said the baron. "But who supervises this agency? Surely, it must be controlled by a higher body."

"We asked very carefully about that," replied Harry, glancing triumphantly at Count Zinn. "It is not connected with any other body. It has its own board that makes all decisions according to its own lights."

"It seems to me a very bad system," said Count Zinn irritably, "because there is no way to correct abuses."

"What do you mean, Count Zinn?" asked the princess.

"Well, what if the staff wastes money? Or what if the agency fails to help the needy in its care? Because there's no higher authority to punish it, these abuses can go on forever. That's why you need a government, to force organizations to behave properly."

Mr. Reade replied. "You are quite right to point out that any group or body may become corrupt, or fail to carry out its announced purposes. Certainly it happens here in Voluntaria,

I must admit. But it is not true that our voluntary agencies face no higher authority. Every group faces public opinion. It faces its donors. It faces its volunteers. It has to behave in an effective, upright way to retain their support. Every day, our newspapers have accounts criticizing this group or that. Each criticism can lead to a loss of support from donors and volunteers, and if the organization doesn't correct its faults, it will soon run out of money and volunteer support, and disappear.

"A good example was the Refugio Welfare Society," he continued. "If you had visited Voluntaria when I was a boy, you would have found that the RWS was the main group helping the needy. It had a huge building down on Rampart Street that I used to pass on my way to school. What happened to it? A reporter uncovered a scandal. You see, the RWS followed the practice of giving handouts of food. People would line up for blocks every Tuesday at noon for the free food that was given away. Well, this reporter—I forget his name—investigated those who were taking the food. He found that some were quite well off and were, in fact, selling the food for money! When the public found out about that, donations to the RWS dropped off dramatically.

"That wasn't the only problem, of course. The entire approach of trying to help the needy by giving them material goods came under attack. Scholars wrote articles about how giveaways undermined the motivation of the poor, and actually kept them dependent, and this matter was discussed in the newspapers for many years. As a result, there was a shift in public opinion against the handout philosophy. In the long run, that's what did away with the RWS. And Craftmasters, of course, with its idea of having people exchange work for food, grew out of that change in attitudes." Mr. Reade took a sip of water.

"But don't think Craftmasters can do what it likes, either," he continued. "For example, several years ago, it came out that a staff member was using some leftover paint from the agency to paint his own house, and there was quite a little scandal about that—trivial as it was. No, our organizations have learned to be very careful about waste or dishonesty even in a small degree. They have learned, as we say, that 'spotless houses have spotless doorsteps.'"

The conversation was interrupted by dessert, which was a huge, cake-like pudding brought from the kitchen by Philippe, who took slow and careful steps so as not to tip it to the least degree. After he set it in the middle of the table, Mrs. Reade took a match and lit a fuse at one side. The entire dessert erupted in a shower of sparks that came from half a dozen flaming pinwheels! Everyone at the table oohed and aahed in amazement.

The shower of sparks quickly ended. "This is called a roly-poly pudding," said Mrs. Reade. "It's a Refugio tradition to serve it at dinners with honored guests." The dessert tasted as good as it looked—although it was rather bouncy and, shall I say, elusive. I found myself having to chase it rather strenuously around the plate with my fork in order to cut it up and eat it.

When we had finished and laid our forks to rest, Mrs. Reade addressed the baron, "And what did you learn about the streets on your expedition with Nathan today?"

"Ah, yes," the baron replied. "As it happened, your husband and I were unable to encounter any overall authority in the matter of public works. The streets, parks, and other facilities are managed by a series of independent groups.

"However"—his voice became firmer—"I did discover a case that proves the advantage of taxation."

"What case is that, Baron?" asked Mr. Reade.

"The collapse of the Penny Bridge that you told me about."

"Oh yes, that. A terrible thing!"

The baron explained the case to us. "They had this bridge—well, it's rebuilt now, quite handsomely—but it collapsed some years ago. The shocking thing is that the engineers for the—what was the name?"

"The Neckar Bridges Consor," said Mr. Reade.

"Yes, the Neckar Bridges Consor. This is the group in charge of this and other bridges on this river. These engineers knew that the bridge was dangerous, is that not so, Mr. Reade?"

"Yes, indeed. They knew it was dangerous, and likely to collapse under extreme loads. And they wrote reports and told everybody, and the Consor had instituted a collection to raise money to reconstruct the bridge."

"But," the baron took up the narrative, "they couldn't raise enough money. So nothing was done and, finally, on one of their feast days—"

"Madge Day," interposed Mr. Reade. "Probably our biggest celebration, with the bridge all crowded with people to watch the boat races—"

"—it collapsed" continued the baron, "killing 12 people and injuring many more."

"Oh, it was dreadful!" said Mrs. Reade, entering the conversation. "And to have that happen on Madge Day, of all days. The whole country was shocked."

"It was sad," agreed the baron, "but it does prove the need for taxation."

"How so, Baron?" asked Mr. Reade.

"Because with taxation, as we have in Pancratica, we would certainly have raised the money to repair the bridge. So you see, son"—the baron turned to Philippe—"that's an example of a public service that requires forcible taxation. I'm surprised," he turned back to Mr. Reade, "that after the collapse of the bridge, there wasn't a move to adopt taxation here?"

"Ah, but that goes against our philosophy, our principle of not initiating force for any reason, not even for a good cause," replied Mr. Reade. After a pause, he continued.

"There's another aspect of the case that you are perhaps overlooking. The collapse of the Penny Bridge was unfortunate, but it taught us a valuable lesson. It was an example of what can happen if people aren't generous. In fact, it has become a motto: 'Remember the Penny Bridge.' We say it to all our children, pointing out that this is what happens when people are selfish.

"That is the way our society works here in Voluntaria. Every failure in any public service teaches this same lesson, that society depends on generosity and cooperation, and that we must try harder in the future to overcome selfishness. In this way, healthy values are continually reinforced, and our culture grows more generous and more neighborly with each generation."

He glanced at his wife and apparently received a silent reproof. "But I ramble on unforgivably. To make amends for boring you, I want to invite you all to be my guests tomorrow night at the Waterworks."

"That sounds excellent," said the baron. "Pray tell, what is it?"

Mrs. Reade replied. "It's an old factory that has been made into a restaurant with the tables among all the old machinery. Philippe loves to go there and"—she winked at the baron, gesturing toward Mr. Reade—"I think there's more than a little bit of the boy in the man."

Dinner at the Waterworks

On the following day, members of our party again went separate ways. The princess, Harry, and Count Zinn went on a walking tour of the city guided by Philippe. The baron was taken by Mrs. Reade to the property registry, for he was convinced that the agency that kept track of the ownership of property would surely be revealed as the true government of Voluntaria. I spent the day at a library—Voluntaria has a number of these, each run by an independent voluntary organization—to study the history of Voluntaria.

Late in the afternoon, we all met at the Waterworks restaurant. The eatery was indeed an exciting place, with great axles, gears, and chains on all sides, and massive millstones turning slowly round in the center of the floor. Mr. Reade pointed out that the millstones were not actually grinding, but were supported and slightly separated by bearings that enabled them to turn freely. "If they were actually grinding, Count Nef, you wouldn't be able to hear yourself think," he said. "I know, because I was inside here once as a boy when the mill was still operating."

We sat down at the table reserved for us. After the bustle of taking seats had subsided, Count Zinn spoke. "In our excursion today, we did not find a government, but we found another problem that government could have solved."

"What is that?" asked Mrs. Reade.

"The Neckar River—why it's terribly polluted with a gray silt that comes, Philippe tells us, from a slate mill in the mountains."

"Ah, yes," said Genna. "We're all so unhappy about that."

"Now in Pancratica, government would have fixed that problem, just like that." Count Zinn snapped his fingers.

"How, Count?" asked Genna.

"By telling the owner he could not pollute the river, and that if he continued to do so, we would put him in jail."

"You certainly do like your jails in Pancratica," Genna said quietly.

"Perhaps so, but at least we have clean rivers!" replied the count.

"Yes, but you are using force to do it," she replied. "That kind of approach would take us back to the Apple Wars, teaching people that it's right to use force. I would rather have dirty rivers than use force against a neighbor."

"You mean that you will just sit and do nothing while your rivers are polluted?"

"Not at all, Count," replied Genna. "There are many things we can do, and are doing, to correct the problem. Journalists have written many articles in the newspapers about it. Public opinion is coming around very strongly on this matter. Why, just the other day, a group of schoolchildren wrote letters to the owner of the slate mill to urge him to stop the pollution. I'm sure he was very embarrassed! One of our associations—it's called the Nature League—is raising money to pay for a purification plant at the slate mill, a plant that the owner can't afford. But all these methods take time."

"In Pancratica, we are not so patient with wrongdoing," said Count Zinn, unwilling to let the matter drop. "We would close the mill and put the owner in jail, and have a clean river the next day!"

"But what about the workers who would lose their jobs?" asked Mrs. Reade.

"And where would we get slates for our roofs if the mill was closed?" asked Philippe.

"There are always going to be these kinds of difficulties," replied Count Zinn with a wave of his hand. "You can't make an omelet without breaking a few eggs."

"Perhaps," Mr. Reade said, "one could say that here in Voluntaria, we don't believe in breaking eggs for any reason." Then, in a lighter tone, he added, "We do, however, believe in omelets, and in eating supper, and here is the waiter to take our orders."

When the orders had been taken, Count Zinn asked the baron, "Well, Baron, we expect to hear that you found the real government of Voluntaria at the property office." There was silence. "Surely you did?"

"I regret to say that I did not," replied the baron. "This property registry office—which they call the 'DBA,' standing for Deeds, Boundaries, and Arbitration—seems to be a private organization. It charges its customers to register property ownership and property boundaries, and when people come to it with disputes over ownership or property lines, it also charges for settling these disputes. It does not appear to be controlled or supervised by any higher agency."

Silence came over the table. Count Zinn fingered his silverware, a frown on his face. "It's obvious," he said, putting his fork down with a thump, "that we should give up trying to find a government by looking for the functions it might perform. It's the wrong approach. Of course you can have schools based on private tuition and donated scholarships. Of course you can have bridges paid for by philanthropists. Any service in society can be performed by private groups, or philanthropists, or commercial organizations. You don't need government for any specific service. No," he continued, "if we are going to find the government in Voluntaria, what we need to do is to define it. Unless we have a definition of government, we can't know what we are looking for."

"A very good point, Count," said the baron. "What, then, is the definition of government?" He looked around the table. For a time, no one spoke.

"Is it the thing that makes decisions in a society?" asked the princess. At once she contradicted herself. "But that won't work, because voluntary organizations make decisions, too."

After more silence, the baron answered his own question. "I think government is the agency that makes laws."

"Why, of course that's it," said Count Zinn. "So," he said, turning to Mr. Reade, "who makes your laws?"

Mr. Reade hesitated. "I don't believe I know that word. What are 'laws'?"

"You haven't heard of laws!" exclaimed the baron in exasperation. "It seems that here in Voluntaria, all the important terms of political science are unknown." He sighed. "What are laws? I suppose you could say they are rules that everyone must obey."

"And . . . ?" Mr. Reade hesitated, apparently reluctant to give offense. "Is force used when people fail to obey these rules?"

"Yes," the baron replied, "what we call laws are rules that are enforced by the threat of some physical punishment administered by policemen and the courts."

"Ah, I see," said Mr. Reade. "Well, then, I don't think we have laws here in Voluntaria."

"Why, that's ridiculous!" said Count Zinn. "You must have laws to regulate proper behavior in a society. Otherwise, everyone would abuse everyone else. You have no idea how stupid and selfish human beings can be when left free to act on their own."

Mr. Reade replied. "It appears, Count, that you do not have much faith in people. Could you give an example, Count, of how abuse would occur?"

"Well, like, like . . ." The count looked around. "Like this restaurant, for example. This restaurant could serve tainted food, which could make people ill. You must have laws against that, a rule that says you go to jail or pay a fine if you have an unsanitary restaurant. In Pancratica, we have laws mandating sanitary conditions in restaurants, and detailed regulations implementing those laws. And we have inspectors who come to each restaurant to see that they are obeyed. Surely you must do this here as well?"

"Let's ask the manager," said Mr. Reade. The manager was called over. "Our visitor wants to know," said Mr. Reade, "whether anybody comes to inspect your kitchen to be sure it is clean and sanitary."

"Oh, yes," replied the manager. "We belong to the VRS and the IIH, and—until just a few weeks ago—PF. You can see their seals of approval on the window. Their inspectors come every few months."

"You see, you see!" said Count Zinn eagerly. "Now we're getting somewhere! These are government inspection agencies."

"Not so fast, my friend," said Harry. He turned to the manager and asked, "Who controls these organizations? Who tells them what to do?"

The manager looked puzzled and turned to Mr. Reade, who answered. "The Voluntaria Restaurant Society is a voluntary organization, with the restaurants as members. The other one, the Independent Institute of Health, has members drawn from the general public. It was founded a number of years ago by doctors who believed that the VRS was being too lenient toward its member restaurants in applying standards of cleanliness."

The baron spoke. "Have we not found an instance of hypocrisy here in Voluntaria? Don't these agencies of inspection violate your philosophy of not using force?"

"How so, Baron?" asked Mr. Reade.

"Well, obviously the inspectors rely on force to compel owners to submit to the inspections, and they use the threat of force to make restaurants do what the inspection agency commands."

"Oh, there's nothing like that here, Baron."

"But what happens if someone chooses not to be inspected?"

"They are dropped from the association. That might hurt their business somewhat, because some customers consider that seal of approval important."

"Except at Julia's Junkyard," said Mrs. Reade, smiling and wrinkling her nose.

"Oh, yes, that's an interesting example," said Mr. Reade, chuckling. "Julia's Junkyard is a restaurant that emphasizes an uncouth ambiance, and serves strange dishes, like—"

"Nathan! Not at meal time!" interrupted Mrs. Reade. She was smiling through her sternness.

"Well anyway, they appeal to customers seeking, shall we say, an extreme dining experience. So they make it a point of pride in not belonging to any sanitary inspection service. Of course, I'm sure they're pretty careful with their food. Their customers enjoy the appearance of eating low, but not the indigestion that goes with the real thing!" He gave a hearty laugh.

"In any case," he continued, "inspectors visit only those restaurants that have voluntarily joined the respective association. And if the demands those inspectors make become too burdensome, then the restaurant can leave the association."

"That's exactly what happened with Perfect Food," said the manager. "Those folks are trying for a high standard, admittedly, but when they came out with six pages of regulations for us to follow, we said it was just too much. We try our best to meet everybody's standards, but some of the things they were asking—like painting the floor twice a year—were just plain silly." After a pause, he added, "PF has just about committed suicide as an organization, because almost all restaurants have dropped out. Now they've retracted those regulations, and apologized, but I think it's too late for the organization to recover its prestige." There was silence as our group pondered this interesting account.

"I think I see why Voluntaria has no red tape," said Count Harry. "The only way you can make human beings respect silly and complicated regulations is through the use of force. Do away with force, and burdensome regulations die of their own weight. In any case," continued Harry, with more satisfaction than was called for, "we have proven again that there is no government in Voluntaria!"

"Not necessarily," said Count Zinn, jutting his chin aggressively at Harry. "I think our definition of government as the institution that makes laws was wrong. We need a definition of government that gets to the heart of things."

"Then what should we look for, Count?" asked the princess.

At that moment, our conversation was interrupted by a trumpet fanfare. All eyes went to the serving door where waiters dressed up in bird costumes were entering with large bouquets of flowers. The waiters separated into three groups, each taking its bouquet to a different table. Then silence descended, as everyone in the room rose and repeated an obviously well-known poem. These were the words:

> *Grains of sand the mountains make,*
> *Droplets the roaring river.*
> *Then large indeed are my two hands*
> *And heart to serve a neighbor.*

After the refrain was said, the entire room broke into applause and cheering.

"Ah, I forgot this was the 27th. That must have surprised you!" said Mr. Reade after we had seated ourselves again.

"Indeed, it did," said the baron. "What was it all about?"

"It's a way of commending outgoing presidents, the leaders of our voluntary groups. These little ceremonies take place on the 27th of each month, in restaurants all over Refugio. Why, tonight alone, there are probably over a dozen. You see, we follow the custom—at least most groups do—of having presidents step down after two or three years of service. That way they don't become overworked—and new people with new ideas can take over. To express appreciation for their service to the group, other members of the voluntary organization invite the outgoing president to a special dinner, as with the three groups here tonight."

"Is everything in Voluntaria done by volunteers?" asked the princess. "Surely there must be some tasks so distasteful that volunteers can't be found who are willing to do them—like repairing the sewers, let us say. What do you do in this case?"

"I think you have misunderstood the name of our country, Princess." replied Mr. Reade. "Our land is called Voluntaria not because everything is done by volunteers, but because we believe in voluntary methods to achieve social aims. Most of our associations have paid employees, such as managers, clerical workers, and technicians.

"Of course, our country does have many, many volunteers. In fact, I would say that practically everyone volunteers in some capacity or other, and usually in more than one organization. And all the presidents of the different associations are always volunteers."

"How do you get people to volunteer?" asked Harry. "We find that most people in Pancratica are too preoccupied with their own affairs."

Mr. Reade thought a moment and then replied. "I think we volunteer here because we understand that civilization depends on it. Without volunteers to promote and manage the voluntary groups that provide services—streets, schools, art museums, and so on—life in this land would be, as one of our philosophers has put it, 'nasty, brutish, and short.'" After a moment, he added, "We also find that volunteering is a personally rewarding activity—perhaps the most rewarding challenge a human being can undertake. Life is an empty and unfulfilling existence when it is lived for self alone. Why—just to give a small example—we would have missed the pleasure of meeting you and learning about your land of Pancratica if Gloria and Philippe had not been volunteers in the Cosmopolitan Society."

"Why are the waiters wearing the bird costumes?" asked the princess, looking at the waiters who were starting to file back into the kitchen.

Philippe answered her. "They are dressed as wrens, because that is the name of the award that the outgoing presidents were given. The Wren. It's named after Douglas Wren, one of the greatest volunteer leaders in our history!"

"He was president of different organizations 74 times," said Genna. "Once, he was president of six at the same time!"

"The actual award," said Mrs. Reade, "is a tiny golden dandelion placed in the middle of each bouquet. Wren was well known for having a vase of dandelions in his little room—he lived a very Spartan life but he always liked to have flowers, especially dandelions, on his table. He said these flowers symbolized voluntary associations—humble, yet beautiful if you pause to look at them closely, and remarkably hardy." After a pause, she added, "That poem we just repeated was one of his."

They were interesting words to ponder as we made our way home under the stars through the quiet streets of Refugio.

The Excursion to Citadel

Breakfast time the next morning was a bustle of excitement. The princess, Count Harry, and I were preparing to travel to Citadel, the ancient city in the interior, and we had our bags to pack, questions to ask, and instructions to write down.

After we had rushed through our breakfast and placed our luggage at the door, we found ourselves with a few moments to spare, as the coach had not yet arrived. The baron took advantage of the pause to ask questions of our host.

"I find it hard to believe," said the baron, "that you do not use force in any way in this country. What about murderers? What about robbers? Do you simply let them go their merry way?"

"No indeed, baron," replied Mr. Reade. "This problem is dealt with by one of the most important groups we have here in Voluntaria. As I have been a member of this organization for many years, I can tell you something about its history and operations."

Genna was just at that moment coming down the stairs. "Oh, yes," she said proudly, "Daddy's very busy with COPS."

"When voluntary communities like Refugio were first formed following the perfection voluntarism of Herbert Herbert," continued Mr. Reade, "the question arose of how to handle aggressors within the community. Members were prepared to defend the city against bands that might attack from the outside, but what about robbers, rapists, or murderers in the city itself? True, those who joined the community had supposedly accepted Herbert's doctrine against the initiation of force, but human beings are imperfect. Some might forget this creed in a moment of anger, or ignore it out of greed. To deal with violent aggression within the city, associations sprang up in each place. Ours is named the Committee of Peace and Safety, but everyone calls it by its initials, COPS."

"Let me see if I understand this," said the baron. "If a person is committing a crime—let us say breaking into a hostelry at night to steal a saddle—members of this COPS would apprehend him?"

"That is correct."

"And drag him away to a jail, or a place of confinement?"

"Yes, if necessary."

"Then, are you not using force, just as we do in Pancratica?"

"I believe there's a difference, Baron," replied Mr. Reade. "COPS is careful to use force only against those who have initiated the use of force. A murderer initiates the use of force. So does a robber, or a rapist. Herbert's philosophy, as I explained the other day, allowed for the use of force against aggressors, in reaction to acts of violence. COPS can never initiate the use of force. In your land, as I understand it, your gopherment *initiates* force against people who haven't themselves used force. For example, in the case of mobbery, the gopherment initiates force against peaceful citizens to compel them to give up money, does it not?"

"It is *taxation*, not mobbery," said the baron with some asperity. "And also, the word is 'government,' not—not what you are calling it."

"I beg your pardon," said Mr. Reade. "Perhaps you would write these words down so I can remember them."

After he had done so, Harry asked a question. "Getting back to the function of this COPS organization, once the wrongdoer has been apprehended, what happens?"

"A confabulation is held, presided over by five judges. They hear the evidence and arguments on all sides about what the accused has done, and then they decide a settlement. For example, in the case of the person who stole the saddle, the judges might decide that the thief should give the saddle back and pay a certain sum to the owner of the hostelry. Generally the settlement includes an apology. Sometimes the transgressor agrees to wear a T-shirt for some length of time."

"What, pray tell, is that?" asked the princess.

Genna answered, "It's a big jacket with the letter 'T' on it that you agree to wear for so many days. So everyone knows you have been a thief. It's a way of apologizing to the public for stealing."

"This sounds very much like our system of justice," said Harry. "But there is one thing I don't understand. Last night, you said there were no laws in Voluntaria. Surely, you need laws to decide these cases."

"Why so, Count?"

"In order to make sure that the same crime is punished equally. In Pancratica, our laws say what the punishment is for each crime. For example, the punishment for stealing a saddle is one year in jail."

"But what is the virtue in equal punishment? Every case is different, and every person is different. The case of a youngster who steals a saddle as a lark is entirely different from that of a habitual thief who steals a saddle. Perhaps the best punishment for the youngster is the T-shirt for a few days, while the habitual thief needs to be sent outland. The judges at each confabulation decide what is best in each case. Their objectives are—just a minute, I saw a very good statement in a book I was reading."

Mr. Reade picked up a book from the side table and quickly found his place. "Yes, here it is—'The aims of the confabulation are threefold: to reduce the likelihood of a future use of force by the offender or others, to minimize the resentment felt by the offender at his treatment, and to limit feelings of anger against the offender by victims and other members of society.' That puts it very well. You see, in each case, we look for the solution that will reconcile all parties, and draw them closer together. In some cases, this means no punishment at all is warranted."

"What is the outland?" asked the princess.

"Oh, I should have explained that," replied Mr. Reade. "That punishment grew up from the old days when the towns would banish wrongdoers to the area lying outside the jurisdiction of the town, which was called 'outland.' When all of Voluntaria was consolidated under control of the various towns, there was no outland left of course, and no place to send those who had committed serious acts of violence. So various groups established outland camps, or compounds of various sorts."

"Yes," said Harry. "At Craftmasters, they told us about the one they operate." He turned to the baron. "The wrongdoer is expected to create everything he needs for life. He is given a tiny tent and a small supply of food when he arrives, and must create everything else. He even has to weave his own clothing if he wants anything more than he stands in. They say it does wonders in boosting the self-confidence of the prisoners—and also leads them to cooperate with each other."

"How interesting!" said the princess. "We should try that in Pancratica."

"Tell me," asked the baron turning to Mr. Reade, "how do you punish murderers? We are having a debate on that subject right now in Pancratica."

"Generally, they would be sent outland for some length of time, although it's difficult to say, we have had so few. In the past ten years, there have only been four murders, and none in the past two years."

"What?" exclaimed the baron. "Why in Pancratica, we have over 15,000 murders every year!"

"How dreadful!" said Mr. Reade. He gave Mrs. Reade a knowing look.

"I wonder why we should have so many more killings in our country?" asked the baron.

Mr. Reade seemed reluctant to reply. "Well, perhaps . . . perhaps that is because in Pancratica you believe in force. You initiate force for all the things you think are good—like regulating restaurants, for example, or mobb—er, I mean, taxation to pay for schools. It seems to me this sets an example to everyone that using force is a proper way to achieve one's goals."

No one replied to Mr. Reade's observation. "Here in Voluntaria," he continued, "we go to great lengths to avoid using force, in order to establish the idea that using force is wrong. Over the years, our people have gradually absorbed this message, and it has now become a basic part of our cultural heritage, so that even individuals who might be angry or deranged hesitate to resort to violence."

"But didn't you just say that your COPS uses force to apprehend wrongdoers?" asked Count Zinn.

"Well, we will use force if we must, Count," replied Mr. Reade, "but we strive to do so only as a last resort—even if it

means risking our lives. We are all volunteers, by the way. No one is paid anything for service to COPS, so that it may never be said that anyone receives any benefit from using force. Furthermore, we normally go unarmed. In this, we follow the example set by Madge Grey."

"Oh, let me tell them about Madge, Daddy!" pleaded Genna.

"Yes, dear, go ahead."

"It happened—" she thought a moment "—over 500 years ago, at one of the last major battles in Voluntaria, just outside the town of Citadel. Both sides had been fighting for many weeks, with neither one nor the other making any headway, but many killed on both sides. Finally, there was a lull in the fighting, and Madge decided to walk out on the battlefield, without any arms or armor, and plead for the men to stop fighting. 'Do you not have wives, sweethearts, daughters, and sons?' That's how her speech began. Practically every child in Voluntaria memorizes it. Anyway, just as she finished her speech, someone shot an arrow that went right into her chest—" Genna shuddered "—and she died right there! The men who were fighting were so moved by the death of this self-less, courageous woman they threw down their arms and walked away from the battlefield! So she stopped the battle without using any arms whatsoever."

"She established the ideal," said Mr. Reade, "that COPS members have tried to follow ever since, the example of avoiding the use of weapons in trying to quell violent situations, even at risk to ourselves. We rely almost entirely on personal physical restraint. Of course, in modern times, there is little danger any more to peace officers, now that the populace has so fully adopted pacific habits. For example, all four of those murderers I just mentioned were remorseful and turned themselves in on their own. Sometimes

I wonder if we today would have the courage of people like Madge and the other early martyrs who walked into really dangerous situations unarmed."

Mr. Reade's comments were interrupted by the arrival of the stagecoach that was to convey us to Citadel. This vehicle, called a "tureena," is unusual in having an outside staircase that leads from the cabin to the driver's seat on top. It thus enables passengers to make their way to and from the driver while the coach is in motion.

We were soon aboard with our luggage stowed, and the prancing horses drew our coach lumbering down the street. I should note that the fare for the journey to Citadel was quite high—312 mintos each person. We were given to understand that this expense was mainly to cover the payments the turnpike association has to make to the various farmers who own the land through which the road passes. As a result of these high payments for land, there are relatively few roads and rather little vehicular traffic between towns in Voluntaria. I could not resist musing that this problem could be overcome if Voluntaria had a government that could seize land for roads from the owners, as we do in Pancratica, but that is not the Voluntaria way. Their approach does have one benefit, I must concede: There is no traffic congestion on the roads.

We arrived in Citadel late in the afternoon, entering this walled city through the massive oaken gates used in olden times to shut up the fortress in times of war. One could see from the encrustation of rust on the hinges that these portals had not been closed for many generations. The coach took us to the house of a local family, volunteers of the VCS (contacted through Mrs. Reade), who were our most amiable hosts.

We paid a visit to a church of the Seekers, the most popular religious sect in Voluntaria. Their creed, as it was explained to us, is that man's knowledge of God is imperfect and continually expanding. Although they do hold various beliefs about God, and God's moral and ethical commands, these are viewed as tentative. Their motto, which we saw elaborately inscribed in several places in this beautiful building, is "Question and Believe." I suspect that such a nondogmatic religion is probably a result of this society's rejection of force. Not able to use violence to compel adherence to any creed, or to punish heresies, the Voluntarians have naturally developed a tolerant style of religion.

On the second day of our stay, our host took us to an unusual athletic contest known as "knights"—a shortened form of its full name, Knights of the Vale of Omatidian. At first, to our eyes, it appeared to be an ordinary variation of scrum football, with two teams tussling to move a ball to opposite ends of the field. But our host drew our attention to a single player, dressed in a distinct red-and-white uniform, standing off to the side, in the middle of the field. This was the "knight," a player completely independent of either team, whose aim is to seize the ball whenever it might come loose during play, and race away with it to his goal, or "keep," at the side of the field. If he succeeds in this, he wins the match outright, and carries away the prize money put up for the match (which on that day was the huge sum of 35,000 mintos). I must say, I found myself much more interested in the doings of the knight than in the actions of the teams. He darted and dodged around the edges of the scrums, always looking for an opportunity to dash in and seize the ball. Twice he got his hands on the ball, but both times the players stripped him of it before he could race away to the keep. Our host reported this outcome was typical, that only about one game in eight ends in a successful plunder. Apart from the excitement it provided us, the game of knights was thought provoking. It appears to be the only game in the entire world that has three "sides." This possibly reflects something of the culture of Voluntaria.

Though the visit to Citadel was stimulating, the greatest excitement occurred on the journey home. Several hours into our journey in the tureena, the princess decided to go up and join the coachman, to view the countryside from his box. She opened the door to the exterior stairway, and closed it behind her. As she was ascending, the coach passed over a rut, giving such a great jolt that the princess was pitched off the stairway! She tumbled through the air, landed on the grassy embankment at the side of the road, rolled head over heels down a slope, and struck her head on a log—a blow that caused her to lose consciousness!

Meanwhile, we in the coach knew nothing of her accident. We assumed she had ridden the rest of the way into Refugio on the top of the coach. And the coachman, for his part, assumed that she was with us. When we arrived back at the Reades', both Harry and I were asleep, catching up on the slumber we had missed during our visit to Citadel. Thus, when we awoke and quitted the coach, we assumed that the princess had long since entered the house.

It was not until suppertime that we noticed her absence. We then concluded that she must have wandered out into the city, and then lost her way. It did not occur to anyone that she had never arrived in Refugio. After consulting with our hosts, we decided to alert the COPS. Soon, a bevy of young officers was combing the riverbanks and forest glades looking for her. At bedtime, they still had found no trace, and we retired deeply worried.

Meanwhile, the princess, after tumbling down the slope and striking her head, lay unconscious for some time. When she awoke,

it was pitch dark. Tall trees loomed over her, shutting out even the light of the stars. The side of her head hurt and she felt stiff and cold. Then she began to think about where she was. What if there were wild beasts in the forest, she wondered, bears, or even larger strange animals in this unusual country? She heard a rustling in the leaves that made her hair stand on end. After a few moments, when nothing more happened, she relaxed slightly, concluding it might have been only a mouse.

Then she saw something that made her gasp in terror. Some distance away through the trees, a light was moving, jerking back and forth, coming toward her. She could see an arm of a person holding this light, shining it along the ground. He was clearly looking for something—or someone! The princess, in her state of anxiety, could hardly avoid the conclusion that he was looking for helpless victims! She lay flat against the ground, trembling, watching the light dart back and forth, moving closer and closer.

Then she suddenly remembered: She was in Voluntaria, the country where people were kind and courteous, where they didn't believe in using force! She realized that whatever this man was up to, he probably didn't pose a threat to her. In fact, he would probably help her. She sat up and cried out. "Hello! Can you help me?"

Now it was the man's turn to be frightened. Hearing an unexpected voice so close by in the dark startled him. His arms flew up and he jerked the lantern over his head. Then he regained his composure and shined the light at the princess. "What's this, what's this?" he said. "Why, my goodness, it's a girl! What are you doing here, dear?"

"I . . . I fell from the coach and was knocked un-, unconscionable. I just woke up."

"Goodness gracious, how awful—and you have cuts all over your arms! You must come back home where my Nayle will patch you up. Can you walk?"

On unsteady legs, the princess rose, with the man holding her arm to help her. Slowly, they made their way through the forest. Soon the princess could make out the glowing windows of a house. As they approached, the man cried out, "Nayle, we have a visitor!"

A woman opened the door. "What . . . ? Oh my!" she said, looking at the princess. "Are you all right?"

The princess was quickly seated by the fire and given a glass of wine and water. Elyan—for that was the man's name— fetched a quilt and put it over her shoulders while Nayle, his wife, cleaned and bandaged her scratched arms. The effect of the wine, along with the shock of the fall—made the princess extremely drowsy. She had hardly time to explain to her hosts who she was and what had happened before she began to nod off. Nayle took her to a bedroom next to the kitchen. "You may sleep here," she said, patting the bed. The princess lay down and Nayle pulled off her shoes, unfolded a quilt upon her, and tiptoed out the door.

When the princess awoke the next morning, she was thoroughly confused, for she had to remember, first, what country she was in, and secondly, that she was lost in that country! But soon it all came back to her—how she had been jolted off the tureena and had come to this home in the forest. She sat straight up in bed and said, "I have to get to Refugio. How worried everybody must be!"

She pushed open the door to the kitchen and saw two little girls and Nayle at the breakfast table.

"Good morning, my dear. How are you? You must be famished!" said Nayle, pulling up a chair for her to sit upon.

In truth, except for a bump on her head that hurt when she touched it, the princess felt quite well. She greeted the wide-eyed and speechless little girls with a cautious smile and said, "Hello," and soon the children were talking to her like an old friend.

Of course, the princess had to retell the story of her accident to the children, and explain where she was from and what she was doing in Voluntaria. As for her return to Refugio, Nayle explained, that had already been planned. Elyan had a load of pigs to deliver in town, and would take the princess there in the cart later in the morning.

"If we seem excited today," continued Nayle, "it's because the inspectors are coming."

"What inspectors are those?" asked the princess.

"The health and safety inspectors from D&D, the Dangers and Diseases Society. Every year, we ask them to come and point out dangers in our house and on the farm. They give us a score on all the things we are doing correctly."

"Last year, we scored 96 percent!" said one of the girls, whose name was Hannah.

"That sounds wonderful," said the princess. "I'm surprised," she continued, turning to Nayle, "that you are eager to see inspectors. In Pancratica, everyone dreads inspectors of all kinds. People will do anything to keep them away."

"That is strange," said Nayle. "I wonder why that should be?"

The princess thought a moment, and then sat bolt upright. "I'll bet it has to do with force!" she said. "It seems that every time we find something different here in Voluntaria, it's because you're against force. Let me see if I can figure it out." Her brow furrowed. "When the inspector comes and finds something wrong, and you *don't* want to change it, what happens?"

"Nothing," replied Nayle, puzzled by the question.

"The inspector doesn't fine you, or put you in jail, or force you to move out of the house?"

"Oh, goodness no. For example, five or six years ago, the inspectors said those cotton window curtains next to the stove"—she pointed to the blue and yellow fabric—"were dangerous because they might catch fire from the heat of the stove. 'Well,' I said, 'maybe they are, but they make a world of difference to this kitchen and I'm not going to take them down!' For years, it cost us a point on our score, and the girls were disappointed about that." She nodded toward the children.

"But now we've got that all settled. Last year, the inspectors showed us how to rinse the curtains in a chemical that keeps them from burning, so they aren't dangerous anymore." Nayle put her hand to the side of her mouth and whispered, "We think we could even get 100 this year!"

"That's the explanation!" interjected the princess. "That's why you want inspectors to come to your farm. Because they can't force you to do anything. They are like friends whose advice you are free to take or ignore. So they can only help you." She paused. "In our country, inspectors compel you to do what they say. Naturally, they are feared and resented. And when their backs are turned, people do what they want anyway. For example, they would put the curtains back up when the inspectors left the house." After a moment, she added, "It seems to me that your voluntary system is more effective in the end."

Shortly after breakfast, Elyan came in and announced that the pigs were loaded and that he was ready to take the princess to Refugio. After affectionate good-byes, she climbed on top of the wagon, and away they went.

As they bounced along the road, the princess asked a question of Elyan, "What were you looking for last night when you found me?"

"Looking for?" His brow furrowed. "Oh, yes," he replied, finally understanding her question. "That must have seemed strange, to see a man coming through the forest shining a light along the ground," he said smiling. "I was looking for night crawlers."

"I beg your pardon?"

"Worms, to go fishing with this morning."

"Oh, my goodness!" she exclaimed. "Something so simple and innocent. You have no idea how afraid I was at first." After a pause, she said, "Fear sprouts in the bog of ignorance—that's what my father says. He's the king of Pancratica."

Deciding the Wager

You can imagine the excitement that greeted the princess's return! We had arisen that morning in a state of despair. The newspapers had carried the story of her disappearance, so everyone in Refugio knew of our plight, and people about the neighborhood wore long looks. Although no one mentioned it, we had each begun to consider the possibility that the princess might not be alive.

Mrs. Reade saw the princess first, just as she was arriving atop the pig cart. She uttered a shout—I think you could almost say it was a scream—of joy. Everyone rushed out the front door to see the princess and help her down.

"How you do manage to get yourself into trouble, dear, no matter where we go!" said the baron, picking her up as he hugged her. Elyan, who was seen as the princess's savior, was greeted almost as warmly.

Later, as we were discussing the accident during lunch, Count Zinn made an observation that led to an interesting revelation about Voluntaria. "You probably have good grounds for a lawsuit, Princess. The design of that tureena is obviously dangerous. Anybody could fall off as you did."

"Oh, Count, don't be silly. It was my own fault for not holding on," said the princess.

"I beg your pardon," said Mr. Reade. "What is a loss suit?"

"A lawsuit," replied Count Zinn, "is when you go to a lawyer who gets you money for damages that you have suffered in an accident or from some other kind of harm."

"Excuse me, but what is a 'lawyer?'"

Count Zinn rolled his eyes and looked over at the baron. "Oh no, here we go again!" Turning back to Mr. Reade, the count continued. "He manages the lawsuit, which is, really, a complaint, saying that this person has hurt you or offended you in some way. If the court agrees, then this person has to pay you money."

"And what happens if he doesn't agree that he is to blame? What happens if he doesn't want to go to this court, or doesn't want to pay the money the court says he should?"

"Oh, well, he must," said Count Zinn. "If he doesn't, policemen will take away his property. They can even put him in jail if he refuses to heed the demands of the lawyers or the judges."

"Ah, I think I see," said Mr. Reade. "In a lawyersuit, a person initiates the use of force to obtain compensation for some grievance, and the lawyers are the agents in this process of using force."

"Well, yes, I suppose you could put it that way," said the count.

After a pause, Mr. Reade said, "I would imagine that these lawyers are not very popular."

"You're certainly right about that," replied the baron, giving a chuckle. "We have many unflattering jokes about lawyers in our country."

"No, we don't have anything like that here in Voluntaria," continued Mr. Reade. "I dare say that if the princess went to the stage-coach company with a complaint, the company would be happy to enlist an arbitrator to suggest a proper settlement, because they want good relations with the public."

"But then how do you punish irresponsible companies?" asked Count Zinn. "I think this tureena ought to be taken off the roads. It's a menace to humanity! In Pancratica, we would accomplish this either by a lawsuit that bankrupts the company with an adverse judgment, or a government regulation forbidding the use of tureenas. That's the way a country with a real government handles these problems."

"But aren't these solutions rather one-sided, Count?" replied Mr. Reade. "Bankrupting the company puts people out of work and ruins the owners. Furthermore, the tureena is a colorful and interesting vehicle. Isn't that an argument for preserving it? If you abolished everything that had any risk or danger, you would be left with a very drab country."

"That's an aspect I hadn't considered," the count conceded.

"Also, don't these forcible approaches make disputants into enemies? If the princess were to try to force the stagecoach company to pay her money in one of these lawyersuits, the owners and managers of the company would draw back in resentment and suspicion. Why, even having this system of lawyersuits in place would make anyone who might have caused an accident reluctant to admit blame and reluctant to apologize, is that not so?"

When the count made no reply, Mr. Reade continued, "And as for punishing irresponsible companies, one shouldn't forget the power of public opinion. I can guarantee you that tomorrow's papers will have a great deal of comment about the princess's accident."

The following day, we saw that Mr. Reade's prediction was correct, for the newspapers carried many articles about the princess's accident, and there were several letters to the editor criticizing the transportation companies for using tureenas. Also, first thing in the morning, the manager of the stagecoach line came to the princess. He was beside himself with apologies, and offered to have a doctor look at her. He also reported that they had devised an ingenious way to prevent such an accident from occurring again. On each tureena, they were going to install a bell on the door to the staircase, which would ring whenever the door opened.

"So," he explained, "when a passenger steps out on the stairs, the driver will know it. Then he will drive slowly and carefully until the passenger reaches the seat beside him." He added, "I'm just so sorry we didn't think of this before your accident."

The princess assured the distraught man that she was recovering well, and that it wasn't the fault of the company in any case.

The morning papers also contained another piece of news, which we heard from Genna as soon as she read it. "They did it! It's going to be fixed!" she shrieked in delight.

"What is it, darling?" asked Mrs. Reade.

"The Neckar. Donald Ducat has made a huge donation to the Nature League, so that along with money the mine owner is putting up, they're going to build a treatment plant for the water at the slate mill. This treatment, it says, will make the water going into the Neckar clean enough to drink! Isn't that wonderful!"

Mrs. Reade saw that we were puzzled. "Donald Ducat is one of the wealthiest men in Refugio, and very generous with his money. Does it say how much he gave, dear?"

"Nine million mintos!" Genna replied.

"Mr. Ducat is also one of the most talented entrepreneurs in the city," said Mr. Reade. "He has created a number of remarkable businesses."

"And also the shoe house!" said Philippe.

"Oh yes," said Mr. Reade. "Tell our guests about that, son."

"He built a house in the shape of a shoe!"

"I don't understand," said the princess. "You mean a house for people to live in, in the shape of a shoe?"

"Yes, exactly that! A big house. It has eleven rooms. I went on the tour!"

"It's quite a story how that house was built," said Mr. Reade. "When Ducat first proposed to build this shoe-shaped house, all the neighbors were opposed to it, saying it would lower property values, and make the district—it's called Eastern Portal—the laughingstock of the city."

"So why couldn't they stop it?" asked Count Zinn. "In Pancratica, they would go to a zoning board and ask them to deny permission to build it."

"Well, there's no need for any such permission here. You can build what you like on your land. So Ducat went ahead. He did a fine and careful job, with lavish gardens and trees planted just so. Well, this shoe house became the talk of the town. Pretty soon everyone was walking up there on Sundays to see it. Sometime later, a neighbor built a house in the shape of a castle, and another neighbor built one to resemble a sailing ship."

"And another is a mouse!" exclaimed Philippe.

"That can't be, can it?" asked the baron.

"Yes, indeed, sir. It even has a tail and whiskers! You must see it."

We made a trip to Eastern Portal that afternoon to see these unusual houses for ourselves. They are not open to the public except on occasional holidays, but the owner of the mouse house made an exception for us, and gave us a complete tour of his fascinating structure. Philippe was quite correct about the whiskers—they were made of stout iron bars, and were a sort of jungle gym for children to swing on.

That evening, the last before our departure, we returned to the subject of deciding whether Voluntaria had a government.

"We still have not arrived at a definition," said the baron. "Count Zinn is right, we can't settle the wager unless we know what a government is. It's something more than just a public body that provides services to the community, or makes up rules, because, as we have seen here in Voluntaria, any number of voluntary groups and commercial organizations can also do that."

A long pause ensued, and then Mr. Reade spoke. "With your permission, perhaps I can suggest a definition?" The baron urged him to continue.

Mr. Reade stretched his arms out on the table. "It seems to me that from the way you talk about it, this government in your country of Pancratica is an agency for using force. That is what makes government different from all other kinds of organizations. It has soldiers and policemen, and it can put people in jail, so it can force people to do things, whereas all the other types of organizations can only ask or persuade or offer money. Therefore, *one* definition might be that government is the agency that publicly uses physical force. Does that not seem correct?"

"Well, then," said Count Zinn, "that means I have won the wager, for here in Voluntaria, you do have such an agency: It is this COPS organization that Mr. Reade has told us about. It uses force against robbers and murderers. Count Harry, your butter treacle is mine!"

"Not so fast, sir!" said Harry, glaring back at him. "The gentleman said that was but one definition of government. Sir," he said, turning to Mr. Reade, "did you have another definition in mind?"

"Well, yes. From the way you speak about government, it seems that in your minds, it is far more than an agency that uses force for the limited purpose of restraining violent aggressors, as our COPS does. It uses force in a positive way, to try and make things better, and to compel people to behave as others think they should. Therefore, this second definition would be that government is the agency that initiates the public use of physical force to attempt to improve society." After a pause, he added, "In this sense, we do not have a government in Voluntaria."

The baron, displaying his diplomatic skill, deftly broke into the conversation before Harry could say a word. "We have, therefore, two definitions of government, one in favor of Count Zinn, and one in favor of Count Harry. I therefore judge the wager to be drawn, with no winner." Both men appeared content with this decision, having, I think, come to the conclusion that one dish of butter treacle at dessert time was sufficient for human happiness.

Our leave-taking the next morning was difficult, with more than one tear shed on both sides. As we pulled away from the dock, with its great crowd of well-wishers waving good-byes, I realized we had made far more genuine friends in this land than in all the other countries of our tour put together. The princess alone had several pages of addresses for correspondents she had promised to write.

———

Several days into our return voyage, during a lunchtime conversation, the princess made a declaration that rather startled us. She had obviously been thinking long and hard about the customs of Voluntaria.

"When I am queen of Pancratica," she said, "I shall abolish all use of force—except to restrain violent people."

"Oh dear, oh dear," said the baron. "That would never do. Why, it would mean doing away with schools and universities, doing away with pensions and health care, doing away with symphonies and scientific research. The people would never permit it. You would be overthrown in a minute! Don't even think of such a thing."

"But, Uncle Koko, that's horrible! Do you mean our entire civilization must continue to depend on force until the end of time? How could I take pride in such a system? How could I consent to be a part of it?"

I don't believe I have ever seen the princess looking so unhappy. No one at the table said anything. After what we had seen in Voluntaria, we knew its system was superior to that which we had in Pancratica, yet, like the baron, we could not imagine putting aside our existing institutions.

"Couldn't I just tell people that force is wrong? Wouldn't they see the truth of that?"

"They are much more likely to think that you are deranged, Princess," replied the baron.

"Then I shall resign the throne and become a hermit!" The princess said this firmly. She was speaking quite seriously.

"Now, now, that will never do," said Harry. "And it would not bring Pancratica one inch closer to being like Voluntaria." He paused and winked at the princess. "And besides, hermits never bathe." The jest, however, failed to cheer her.

Count Zinn spoke. "It's utopian to expect Pancraticans to embrace voluntarism. As the baron says, all our institutions are based on force. They've lasted hundreds of years, and no one can change them. You might as well get used to it."

"I don't believe you are correct, Count Zinn," said Harry. "Institutions do change, although it's bound to be a gradual process. Even in Voluntaria, it took hundreds of years for them to forsake the use of force. I think the same evolution is taking place in Pancratica. For example, years ago, our rulers followed the practice of hanging writers and printers for criticizing the government. We don't do that any more—so there's an example of progress in reducing the use of force."

"That's quite correct," said I. "Also, we already have many voluntary organizations that perform public services, just as in Voluntaria. So it's not as if we didn't know how to address problems without relying on the use of force."

The princess brightened. "Yes, I see! We *are* making progress, only we are very far, far behind Voluntaria." She thought for a moment. "When I am queen, I will find ways to nudge this process of improvement along, so that our society relies less and less on force as time goes by!"

"A very sound approach, Princess," said Harry. "Ah, here comes our dessert of butter treacle." He looked at Count Zinn. "And if we are to transplant the system of Voluntaria to Pancratica, we should bring along Voluntaria's spirit of courtesy, too." He paused. "*Bon appétite,* Count Zinn. May you enjoy the eating of your butter treacle!" He extended his hand to the count, who took it with pleasure.

It was the first time in my life that I had seen these gentlemen shake hands.